THE HEART HEALTHY COOKBOOK FOR BEGINNERS

1500 Days of Easy & Delicious Low-fat and Low Sodium Recipes to Lower Your Blood Pressure and Cholesterol Levels. Includes 30-Day Meal Plan

Laura Kelley

GET YOUR BONUS NOW!

Hello! First of all, I would like to thank you for purchasing "The Heart Healthy Cookbook for Beginners." I'm sure it will be very useful to improve your heart health and overall well-being!. To prove my gratitude for the trust you have placed in my experience, I am so happy to gift you with another one of my books, "MEDITERRANEAN DIET COOKBOOK,"
which I am sure will make your health explode. Don't wait any longer, follow the instructions below to download the digital version for free! Enjoy your reading!

MEDITERRANEAN DIET COOKBOOK
800 Quick, Easy, and Mouthwatering Recipes with Easy-to-Follow Instructions to Help You Weight Loss and Regain Vitality.
30-Day Meal Plan Included

The bonus is **100% free**, with no strings attached.
You don't need to enter any details except your name and email address.

To download your bonuses scan the QR code below or go to

https://books-bonuses.com/laura-kelley-bonuses-hh

Table of Contents

Introduction

With the current changes in the world of health and fitness, people are looking for ways to help them maintain optimum heart and body functions. The guideline is meant to help people shift toward a dietary change that contains more fruits and vegetables and eat lean proteins and whole grains instead of refined processed foods. Based on recent evidence, there is a direct correlation between the cholesterol in the blood and the type of food that is consumed. Foods rich in low-density lipoproteins will increase the cholesterol level in the system. However, dieticians and doctors have had to urge people to consume high-density lipoproteins, which are good fats for the body. It is important to note that the body still needs fats; therefore, you need to consume the correct type of fats that will boost the body's functionality without increasing cholesterol levels.

So, what do experts recommend when it comes to heart-healthy eating? For cardiovascular disease prevention, it is recommended that you should consult a dietary pattern that emphasizes the consumption of low-fat dairy products, whole grains, legumes, poultry, fish and nuts. You should limit sugar-sweetened beverages, sweets, and red meats, and your healthy diet must:

- Limit intake of saturated fat intake to 5% to 6% of total calorie intake
- Reduce calorie intake of trans fats and saturated fats
- Maintain your sodium intake to less than 2300 mg to 1500 mg daily for people prone to cardiovascular diseases.
- Limit the intake of added sugars to at least 10% of the total calories consumed daily.

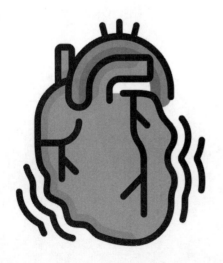

Implementing this eating pattern will likely reduce your chances of cardiovascular disease. It is important to note that the dietary patterns in this book are not fads or diets but a healthy diet plan based on scientific evidence on decreasing the risk of chronic diseases. It is all about the interaction of many antioxidants, minerals, vitamins and phytochemicals that are critical in boosting the functionality of the body cells.

This heart-healthy cookbook is loaded with various simple, healthy, and delicious recipes starting from healthy breakfast choices and ending with delicious desserts. The ingredients used in this cookbook are simple and easily available at your local grocery shop. The book will guide you to change your daily lifestyle toward healthy eating.

What is a Heart Disease?

Any health disorder that affects heart health and its functioning is defined as heart disease. It is also known as cardiovascular disease, which affects the heart and blood vessels. Heart disease starts with depositing the bad fats into the inner wall of arteries, which supply blood to our heart. In this condition, the artery walls get thickened, and hardening also narrows them and restricts the blood flow; this condition is known as arteriosclerosis. As a result, the blood cannot pass freely from these arteries, increasing the risk of heart attack or stroke.

The fats stored in the arteries are in the form of cholesterol. There are different forms of cholesterol known as HDL and LDL cholesterol. HDL cholesterol is good cholesterol; it reduces the cholesterol in the blood and returns it to the liver. The LDL cholesterol is bad; it sticks inside the blood vessels and is sometimes responsible for blocking the blood flow.

Causes and Symptoms of Heart Diseases

There are many causes of cardiovascular disease that affect your heart health. The causes of heart disease include.

- Born with congenital heart defects.
- Coronary artery disease is also known as blood vessel disease.
- Increased blood cholesterol.
- Family history of cardiovascular disease.
- Type-II diabetes.
- High blood pressure.
- Smoking, obesity, metabolic syndrome, stress, lack of exercise, etc.

Heart disease symptoms depend on your type of CVD or heart disease. Some of them include

- **Heart Arrhythmias:** This is a condition in which sometimes heartbeats are too quick or too slow. Abnormal heartbeats are noticed; some causes include flapping in your chest, running heartbeats, slow heartbeats, near fainting, discomfort, dizziness, chest pain, etc.
- **Congenital heart defects:** This heart condition is present at birth due to the complex structure of the heart. Some symptoms and signs in an infant child include swelling around the eye, leg, and abdomen. Also, notice the shortness of breath, etc.
- **Heart Cardiomyopathy:** This condition is challenging to identify because there are no symptoms at an early stage. When the condition worsens, the symptoms include irregular heartbeats swelling in the feet and ankles, fatigue, dizziness, lightheadedness, etc.
- **Endocarditis Infection:** This type of infection affects the inner lining of the heart valves and chambers. Heart infection includes dry cough, fever, shortness of breath, rashes on the skin, changed heart rhythm, swelling, etc.
- **Valvular heart disease:** There were four valves in the heart, including tricuspid, mitral, aortic, and pulmonary valves. There are various causes of damaged heart valves. The sign and symptoms of valvular heart disease include irregular heartbeats, fatigue, chest pain, fainting, etc.

How Is Heart Disease Treated?

Lifestyle adjustments are part of the treatment for coronary artery disease. Do not smoke. Consume plenty of fruits, veggies, and fiber-rich meals. Sugary meals should be avoided. Regular exercise is essential. Keep a healthy weight.

Medicines: Cholesterol-lowering statins, High blood pressure. Drugs Aspirin or other blood clot-prevention meds, Diabetes medications, nitrates, beta-blockers, and other medications used to relieve chest discomfort (angina).

Surgery: Bypass surgery, stenting (also called coronary artery bypass grafting or CABG)

Medications such as calcium channel blockers and anticoagulants treat arrhythmia (blood thinners). In addition, ablation, cardioversion, implantable devices such as implantable cardioverter defibrillators (ICDs), and pacemakers are all options.

Drugs, angiotensin-converting enzyme (ACE) inhibitors, angiotensin receptor blockers (ARBs), anti-arrhythmic medications, antibiotics, anticoagulants (blood thinners), and beta-blockers are used to treat heart valve disease. Diuretics Vasodilators Surgery Valve replacement or repair of the heart valve

Who Should Follow The "The Heart Healthy Eating Pattern"

A heart-healthy eating pattern is essential because there are other benefits of taking this diet apart from a healthy lifestyle. The people following this heart-healthy eating pattern are those who:

- Have metabolic syndrome
- Are on their menopause or post menopause
- Have high levels of triglycerides
- Have excess weight in the middle or belly fat
- They are known to have a polycystic syndrome
- Are prone to diabetes or hypertension

It is imperative to note that when you are taking whole foods, a plant-based diet that includes a daily change of habits and exercises will go a long way in boosting your overall body health.

1. Benefits

The heart plays a significant role in keeping the body working as it should. The heart is a pump that pumps life through the body. The heart has two main functions. It sends blood to the lungs to produce oxygen and then sends that oxygen into the bloodstream and carries it throughout the other parts of the body.

The heart is made up of muscle, and you need to keep active to keep its good conditioning. When your heart is in the best condition, the body functions like a highly maintained engine of a car; it works impeccably. A healthy heart and well-taken care of are more capable of coping with stress and demands on the body. As our body was intended to be active, constant physical activity keeps the heart healthy.

So, it's a brilliant idea to ensure it is healthy and maintain it all the time.

Having a healthy heart will give you more chances to do many things. Having a healthy heart benefits a person on both physical and emotional levels. Aside from these benefits, below are some other benefits you can get from having a healthy heart:

a. *You'll Be Generally Healthier*

Having a healthy heart makes you feel great inside and directly affects how you would appear on the outside. So, a healthy heart will improve your overall fitness levels and make you look better physically.

b. *Make You More Physically Active*

The healthier your heart is, the more active you'll be. It enhances the blood flow, which nourishes all major organs that develop your general fitness. It also gives you more energy for the day. Having a healthy heart also keeps you more ready to throw yourself into physical activities, which keep you fit and active.

c. *Saves You Money*

Keeping your heart healthy can save you much money. For example, the medical expenses related to treating heart illnesses are growing to the point where they're becoming expensive. But you can avoid these expenses by ensuring that your heart stays healthy and spending your money on something else you'd enjoy.

d. *Allows You to Live Longer*

There's no complete assurance that having a healthy heart will make you live your life longer. But checking the rates of people who die because of heart disease, it's safe to say that keeping a healthy heart and in excellent condition can improve your chances to live longer and get you more out of life.

e. *Make you Enjoy Life More*

The effects of heart disease, whether it's the feared heart attack, chest pains, or angina, can stop you from having an active life. If you experience a heart attack, you must be more careful about most things you do to ensure that it doesn't happen again. If you get a coronary bypass operation, this could also need a long time to pull through and put a spanner to make you enjoy your life and have fun again. But if you keep your heart healthy and go for healthier lifestyles, the chances of this happening will get much smaller.

Tips And Tricks To Stick To This Eating Pattern

Three dietary patterns (Mediterranean, DASH, and vegetarian/vegan) have been shown to improve cardiac outcomes, and they have many more similarities than differences. Here are the core components to aim for:

a. *Base Your Meals On Vegetables, Fruits, Or Both.*

This isn't a new idea, but it's still a challenge for most people. Ideally, vegetables and fruit should make up about half of every meal and snack; if that's not realistic for you, start with a little and build from there.

b. *Eat Legumes, Nuts, And Seeds On Most Days.*

Legumes include lentils, chickpeas, dried peas, and beans. Tofu, made from soybeans, counts, too. Experiment with nut and seed butter, from peanut butter to tahini. These plant-based-protein foods have consistently been tied to improvements in cardiac risk factors and outcomes.

c. *Choose Mostly Whole Grains.*

All three dietary approaches include a moderate intake of grains, mostly whole. Bread products are a start, but challenge yourself to try intact grains like oats, quinoa, and barley, which can be cooked without salt and are generally easier on your blood sugar.

d. *Make Extra-Virgin Olive Oil Your First Choice.*

Extra-virgin olive oil is a feature of the Mediterranean diet. However, it makes sense no matter which approach you use, unless you're cooking at very high temperatures for a long time, as when searing meat, stir-frying, or roasting in the oven at 400°F or higher. Heart-healthy oils that withstand high temperatures better include canola, sunflower, grapeseed, and avocado.

e. Aim For At Least Two Servings A Week Of Fish.

Fatty fish, including salmon, trout, and sardines, are especially beneficial.

These three well-studied dietary patterns are all variations of the themes I've just listed. Beyond these general principles, there's more flexibility than you might think.

Mediterranean

The Mediterranean diet is a general eating pattern practiced differently around the Mediterranean region. In addition to the core components just outlined, it's characterized by a wine with meals—although the relative importance of this is unclear. Wine's small potential cardiac benefits should be weighed against the considerable risks of excess. For example, moderate amounts of alcohol are associated with increased breast cancer risk.

Otherwise, Mediterranean diets are typically more fat than the other two, but most of them come from fish, olive oil, and nuts. Red meat is consumed infrequently, and poultry, eggs, and dairy make weekly rather than daily appearances. The Mediterranean lifestyle also involves slowing down to enjoy meals with others and getting plenty of physical activity.

Dash

The Dietary Approaches to Stop Hypertension (DASH) eating pattern was first popularized after two well-designed studies looked at its effect on blood pressure in the late 1990s. Since then, it has been studied extensively relative to other aspects of cardiac health, with consistently positive results.

The diet is high in vegetables and fruit—8 to 10 servings a day for typical adults—as well as whole grains, nuts, seeds, legumes, and mostly low-fat milk products. Meat, fish, chicken, eggs, and vegetable oils are included, but in smaller amounts than is typical in the standard American diet.

Since the original studies, researchers have varied the DASH pattern and seen similarly positive results. One study looked at higher-fat milk products. One reduced carbohydrates slightly and replaced them with more plant-based protein or healthy fats.

The bottom line is that, as long as you include the core components, you can vary the specifics per your preferences.

Vegetarian/Vegan

Thanks to passionate researchers, dramatic documentaries, and concerns about environmental sustainability and animal welfare, there is a great deal of interest in vegetarian and vegan diets. Vegetarians do not eat any meat, including chicken and fish. Vegans go a step further and don't eat any food of animal origin, from dairy products to eggs and even honey.

Evidence tying these approaches to cardiac outcomes is limited but promising. Cardiologist Dean Ornish showed a reversal of atherosclerosis (an arterial disease characterized by deposits of fatty materials) in people randomly assigned to a very low-fat, nearly vegan diet, along with smoking cessation, stress management, and moderate exercise. Atherosclerosis in the control group got worse.

Although the degree of reversal was small, the clinical effect was significant, showing that people in the control group were twice as likely to experience a cardiac event during five years of follow-up. However, because this was a small study and participants did more than just change their diet, we can't say for sure that a low-fat vegan diet is the only way to reverse atherosclerosis. If a vegan diet appeals to you, consider consulting a registered dietitian nutritionist to ensure you meet all of your nutrient needs.

Low-Carbohydrate

Various low-carbohydrate diets have surged in popularity, from Atkins to paleo, South Beach, to the currently popular ketogenic diet. Even the rise in gluten-free eating was driven by a low-carb undercurrent and legitimate gluten intolerance among a small percentage of people.

These diets are popular because they typically result in rapid, although usually temporary, weight loss and the improvement in cardiac risk factors—such as type 2 diabetes, blood pressure, and cholesterol—that go with it. Unfortunately, as noted earlier, weight loss usually returns.

Given that we have few studies examining these approaches beyond two years and none showing reductions in cardiac events or improved mortality, I don't typically recommend them. If, however, such an approach appeals to you, and you think you can realistically eat that way long-term, it is possible to take a heart-healthy approach. Load up on nonstarchy vegetables, nuts, seeds, avocado, fish, and lean meat. Consider working with an RDN to ensure you meet your nutritional needs.

Foods To Eat

Fruits & Vegetables: These are good sources of essential vitamin nutrients, antioxidants, and dietary fibres. The dietary fibers help to lower your blood pressure level and cholesterol. It also improves your blood vessel functions and reduces the risk of heart disease. Seasonable fruits and vegetables are good options available. Fresh fruits are a good source of potassium, magnesium, beta-carotene, and fiber.

Fruits and vegetables include:

- Leafy greens such as spinach, lettuce, collards, Swiss chard, and kale are used as salads.
- Cabbage, carrots, tomatoes, cauliflower, broccoli, etc.
- Fresh fruits include oranges, apples, pears, bananas, cantaloupes, papaya, and peaches. You can also use frozen, canned & dried fruits with no added sugar.

Whole Grains, cereals, and bread: Whole grains are power-packed with iron, magnesium, phosphorus, vitamin B, selenium, dietary fibers, and antioxidants. The dietary fibers help control the blood cholesterol level and high blood pressure. Adding 25 grams of whole grains daily into your diet helps to reduce the risk of heart disease by 15 percent. Whole grains like oatmeal & brown rice help to increase the good cholesterol HDL level and lower the bad cholesterol LDL level.

Whole Grains, cereals, and bread include:

- Cereals with no added sugar, such as shredded wheat and oatmeal, are one of the best choices for hot and cold breakfasts.
- Whole oats, millet, barley, quinoa, buckwheat, bulgur and brown or rice are good for heart health.
- Whole grain bread, bagel, tortillas, and English muffins.

Fat-free or low-fat dairy products: Two daily servings of dairy products helps to reduce the risk of heart disease. A fat-free dairy diet is one of the healthy options available. Hemp milk is a good source of 0mega-3 fatty acids and alpha-linolenic acid. It also contains potassium, vitamin A, vitamin D, and calcium.

Dairy products include:

- Low-fat or fat-free milk
- Soymilk, low-fat yogurt, low-fat cheese, low-fat cottage cheese, etc.

Nuts and seeds: Nuts and seeds are power-packed with heart-healthy oils like omega-3 with protein, fibers, vitamins, and minerals. Nuts and seeds contain unsaturated fats, which help reduce the risk of heart disease.

Nuts and seeds include:

- The best nut choices for a heart-healthy diet are walnuts, peanuts, pistachio, almond, and pecans.

Lean Protein: The number of studies shows that replacing high-fat meat with lean protein helps lower your blood pressure level and increase the good cholesterol in your body. Lean protein has various benefits; it helps build your body muscles and lose extra weight. Adding some portion of lean protein a day will keep you healthy and reduce the risk of heart disease.

Lean Protein includes:

- In seafood fish and shellfish,
- Poultry, turkey breast, skinless chicken, ground chicken, or turkey.
- In pork leg, tenderloin, or shoulder.
- Black beans, kidney beans, lima beans, pinto beans, chickpeas, black-eyed peas, lentils, and split peas in Beans and peas.
- Nuts, seeds, egg white, peanut butter, almond, and tofu.

Healthy oil and fats: Those oil and fats are in liquid form at room temperature and are suitable for heart health compared with solid state. Most of the study and research shows that olive oil is one of the heart-healthy fats. It is a good source of monounsaturated and polyunsaturated fats with omega-3 fatty acids, which help protect you from heart diseases. In addition, it helps to increase the good cholesterol HDL level and decrease the bad cholesterol LDL level. Trans fats & saturated fats are unhealthy fats, increasing the risk of heart disease. These fats are solid at room temperature. Use all oils in moderation.

Healthy oil and fats include:

- Vegetable oils like sunflower oil, peanut oil, safflower oil, canola oil, soybean oil, olive oil, corn oil, etc.

Food To Avoid

Excess sodium and saturated fat intake increase your blood pressure and cholesterol level. Therefore, avoid foods that are high in sodium and saturated fats.

- Foods and beverages with excess sugar: High sugar consumption can raise your blood pressure and increase chronic inflammation. Excess sugar is also responsible for raising your blood sugar level, weight gain, and increasing the risk of heart disease. Avoid extra sugar to maintain a healthy body weight and reduce the risk of heart disease. Instead, use dried fruits in your dish, which helps you sweeten your dish. The American dietary guidelines include less than 10% added sugar in the daily diet.
- Avoid red and processed meat: High red meat intake will increase your heart disease risk. Eating 100g of red meat daily increases the risk of stroke and heart disease by 10 to 20%. Processed meat contains a high amount of salt and preservatives.
- Foods contain high cholesterol: High-fat meat is one of the sources of high cholesterol contents. Consuming high cholesterol food for a longer time increases cholesterol levels and triglycerides in the blood. Most excess cholesterol is stuck inside the blood vessels and arteries and reduces the blood supply, which increases the risk of heart attack or stroke. Avoid red meat such as pork, steak, ribs, and beef—processed meat such as bacon, sausage and hot dogs. Also, avoid fried food, eggs, and shellfish because it contains unhealthy saturated fats.

- Processed foods: A highly processed food contains unhealthy foods such as sodium, sugar, and fats. All these contents make food taste better but increase the risk of health issues like obesity, high blood pressure, blood sugar level, and heart disease. Processed food includes deep-fried food, candy, sugary cereals, sweetened juices, soft drinks, margarine, cookies, pastries, etc.

- Refined Carbs: Refined Carbs: are simple or bad Carbs: high in sugar and responsible for increasing blood sugar levels. They are low in fiber, vitamin, and nutrients, meaning refined Carbs has empty calories. These Carbs: are easy to digest and have a high glycemic index. As a result, refined Carbs: rapidly spike blood sugar and blood insulin level after your meal. Avoid refined-carb food such as white bread, pastries, biscuits, rice cake, spaghetti, white flour, pizza dough, and breakfast cereals.

- Sodium (Salt): Consuming too many salts in the diet increases blood pressure and the risk of cardiovascular disease. According to American Heart Association lowering daily sodium intake to 1000 mg will help reduce your blood pressure level. Also, always read the labels while choosing your food ingredients and choose whole and nutrient-rich food whenever possible.

- Alcohol: Excess alcohol leads to increased blood pressure, in some cases, heart failure or stroke. Too much alcohol consumption can cause irregular heartbeats, also known as arrhythmias. Those who consume alcohol consume it moderately. One drink per day for females and two drinks per day for males.

CHAPTER 2: Breakfast

2. Red Velvet Beet and Cherry Smoothie

Preparation time: 5 minutes

Cooking time: 0 minutes

Servings: 2

Ingredients:

- 1½ cups plain nonfat Greek yogurt
- 1 cup unsweetened almond milk
- 2 tablespoons unsweetened cocoa powder
- 1 cup frozen cherries
- ⅔ cup frozen banana slices
- ½ cup raw peeled and chopped beets
- ½ cup gluten-free rolled oats
- 2 pitted Medjool dates
- 1 teaspoon vanilla extract
- 1 cup ice cubes

Directions:

1. Mix the ingredients in a high-speed blender and blend until smooth.
2. Pour into two tall glasses and serve immediately.

Per serving: Calories: 349kcal; Fat: 4g; Carbs: 65g; Protein: 17g

3. Muesli with Berries, Seeds, and Nuts

Preparation time: 5 minutes

Cooking time: 30 minutes

Servings: 4

Ingredients:

- 1 cup rolled oats
- 1 cup sunflower seeds
- ½ cup chopped almonds
- Pinch of salt to taste
- 1 tablespoon extra-virgin olive oil
- 2 cups unsweetened almond milk
- 2 cups berries

Directions:

1. Preheat the oven to 300 degrees F. Line a baking sheet with parchment paper.
2. Combine the oats, sunflower seeds, almonds, and salt on the prepared baking sheet. Mix well.
3. Drizzle with the oil, and stir well. Spread the mixture in a thin layer.
4. Transfer the baking sheet to the oven, stirring once halfway through, for 30 minutes, or until the muesli is lightly browned. Remove from the oven.
5. Set aside to cool. Serve the muesli with almond milk and berries.

Per serving: Calories: 460kcal; Fat: 32g; Carbs: 34g; Protein: 14g

4. Berry, Walnut, and Cinnamon Quinoa Bowl

Preparation time: 5 minutes

Cooking time: 20 minutes

Servings: 2

Ingredients:

- ½ cup quinoa
- 1 cup unsweetened almond milk
- 1 teaspoon cinnamon, plus more for coating
- 10 raw walnuts
- 1 cup strawberries, sliced

Directions:

1. Preheat the oven to 425 deg. F then line a baking sheet with parchment paper. Bring the quinoa, almond milk, and cinnamon to a boil in a medium pot.
2. Low the heat to a simmer, then cover for 12 minutes, or until the almond milk has been absorbed.
3. Put the walnuts and a dash of cinnamon onto the prepared baking sheet and bake for 5 minutes until lightly golden.

4. In a serving bowl, combine the quinoa and walnuts, and top with the strawberries. (When storing, put the quinoa only in the refrigerator for up to 1 week. Add the walnuts and strawberries when ready to eat.)

Per serving: Calories: 268kcal; Fat: 11g; Carbs: 36g; Protein: 9g

5. Peach-Cranberry Sunrise Muesli

Preparation time: 10 minutes

Cooking time: 0 minute

Servings: 1

Ingredients:

- ⅓ cup vanilla soy milk
- 3 tablespoons rolled oats
- 1 tablespoon chia seeds
- 1 tablespoon buckwheat (optional)
- 1 peach
- 1 tablespoon dried cranberries
- 1 tablespoon sunflower seeds

Directions:

1. Mix the soy milk, oats, chia seeds, and buckwheat (if using) in a large bowl. Soak for at least 10 minutes (and as long as overnight).
2. Meanwhile, cut the peach into bite-size pieces.
3. When the oats have softened up, sprinkle with the cranberries, sunflower seeds, and peach chunks.

Per serving: Calories: 361kcal; Fat: 11g; Carbs: 59g; Protein: 13g

6. Creamy Oats Banana Porridge

Preparation time: 10 minutes

Cooking time: 5 minutes

Servings: 1

Ingredients:

- ¼ cup steel-cut oats
- 1 tbsp peanut butter
- ½ tsp vanilla
- ½ tbsp chia seeds
- ½ banana, mashed
- ½ cup unsweetened almond milk
- 1 cup water

Directions:

1. Add oats & water to a saucepan and bring to boil.
2. Once oats begin to thicken, add vanilla, chia seeds, mashed banana, and almond milk and cook over low heat for 5 minutes. Stir constantly.
3. Top with peanut butter and serve.

Per serving: Calories: 323kcal; Fat: 16.6g; Carbs: 37.6g; Protein: 9.6g

7. Orange Apricot Muesli

Preparation time: 15 minutes

Cooking time: 0 minute

Servings: 4

Ingredients:

- 2 cups regular rolled oats, toasted if desired
- ⅓ cup oat bran
- ⅓ cup dried chopped apricots
- ¼ cup chopped walnuts
- Pinch salt
- 1 teaspoon ground cinnamon
- ¼ cup orange juice
- 1⅓ cups low-fat almond or soy milk

Directions:

1. Mix the oats, oat bran, apricots, walnuts, salt, and cinnamon in a medium bowl. Add the orange juice and milk and mix.
2. Let this stand for 10 minutes, then serve, or cover the bowl and refrigerate overnight, stirring gently before serving.

Per serving: Calories: 280kcal; Fat: 9g; Carbs: 47g; Protein: 9g

8. Strawberry Yogurt Tarts

Preparation time: 15 minutes

Cooking time: 0 minute

Servings: 5

Ingredients:

- ½ cup pitted Medjool dates
- ½ cup crushed almonds
- 1 tablespoon maple syrup
- 1 cup low-fat plain Greek yogurt
- ½ cup strawberries
- 2 tablespoons water

Directions:

1. Line 5 cups of a muffin tin with paper liners and set aside.
2. In a food processor or blender, place the dates and pulse for 10 to 20 seconds until they become a paste.
3. Add the crushed almonds and maple syrup to the blender and pulse to mix.
4. Evenly divide the date mixture into the lined cups and press it firmly; it should fill about one-third of the cup.
5. Blend the yogurt, strawberries, and water in a clean blender until smooth.
6. Pour the fruit and yogurt mixture into the cups until each one is full.
7. Bring the cups to the freezer for 2 hours to set and serve.

Per serving: Calories: 141kcal; Fat: 5g; Carbs: 20g; Protein: 5g

9. Hummus and Date Bagel

Preparation time: 3 minutes

Cooking time: 5 minutes

Servings: 1 bite

Ingredients:

- 1 bagel
- ¼ serving of Homemade Hummus or store-bought hummus
- 6 dates, pitted and halved
- Dash of salt and pepper
- ¼ cup diced tomatoes
- 1 tbsp. chives
- Squeeze lemon juice
- 1 handful sprouts

Directions:

1. Split the bagel in half. Toast the bagel in a toaster or under the broiler.
2. Rub the hummus on each side.
3. Top with the dates, salt, pepper, tomatoes, chives, lemon juice and sprouts.

Per serving: Calories: 410kcal; Fat: 2g; Carbs: 59g; Protein: 91g

10. Peanut Butter Brazilian Nut Smoothie Bowl

Preparation time: 5 minutes

Cooking time: 0 minute

Servings: 2

Ingredients:

- 1 cup coconut milk
- ½ cup canned peanut butter purée
- 1 tsp. pumpkin pie spice
- 2 (1-gram) packets of stevia
- ½ tsp. vanilla extract
- Pinch salt
- ½ cup chopped Brazilian nuts

Directions:

1. Whisk the coconut milk, peanut butter purée, pumpkin pie spice, stevia, vanilla, and salt (or blend in a blender).
2. Spoon into two bowls. Serve topped with chopped Brazilian nuts.

Per serving: Calories: 292kcal; Fat: 23g; Carbs: 15g; Protein: 9g

11. Quinoa Bowl with Blackberry

Preparation time: 20 minutes

Cooking time: 20 minutes

Servings: 4

Ingredients:

- 2 tsps. canola oil
- Nutmeg
- ¾ cup quinoa
- ½ orange, peeled
- ½ cup nonfat milk
- 1 cup water
- 1 tsp. vanilla
- 2 cups fresh blackberries

Directions:

1. Rinse the quinoa and drain. Heat the oil in a medium-sized non-stick pan, add the quinoa, and roast the quinoa on medium-high heat for about 1 minute, stirring constantly.
2. Cut the peeled oranges into small pieces and remove all seeds. Add a little nutmeg and processed oranges to the quinoa, stir and then add water.
3. Simmer on low heat for about 11 minutes until the quinoa is almost soft but still a bit crispy in the middle. Add milk, blackberries and vanilla, stir gently, and simmer for 2 or 3 minutes until the quinoa grains are translucent.
4. Remove from the pot to a bowl and enjoy while it is hot!

Per serving: Calories: 271kcal; Fat: 4.53g; Carbs: 51.83g; Protein: 7.29g

12. Breakfast Cereal with Apples and Raisins

Preparation time: 15 minutes

Cooking time: 15 minutes

Servings: 4

Ingredients:

- ½ tsp. cinnamon
- ⅛ tsp. nutmeg
- 1 tbsp. flaxseed oil
- 2½ cups (600 ml) low-fat almond or rice milk, fortified, unsweetened
- ½ cup whole-grain buckwheat
- ¼ cup apples, coarsely chopped
- 1 tbsp. golden raisins

Directions:

1. Let the milk simmer over medium heat. Add buckwheat to it.
2. Reduce heat to low, gently simmer and cook for approximately 10 minutes, partially covered and stirring frequently, or until the milk is completely absorbed. Remove from heat.
3. Add apples and raisins, then allow the mixture to rest for 5 minutes.
4. Stir in nutmeg, flaxseed oil and cinnamon. Serve.

Per serving: Calories: 133kcal; Fat: 4.6g; Carbs: 18.8g; Protein: 1.8g

13. Cereal Cream with Flaxseed and Fruit

Preparation time: 15 minutes

Cooking time: 15 minutes

Servings: 4

Ingredients:

- 2½ cups (600 ml) almond or rice milk, unsweetened low-fat
- ½ cup whole-grain buckwheat
- ¼ cup apples, coarsely chopped
- 1 tbsp. golden raisins

- ½ tsp. cinnamon
- ⅛ tsp. nutmeg
- 1 tbsp. flaxseed oil

Directions:

1. Heat the pan over medium heat, put in the milk and let it simmer. Add buckwheat.
2. Reduce heat to low, gently simmer and cook partially covered and frequently stirring for about 10 minutes, or until the milk is completely absorbed. Set aside.
3. Add apples and raisins to the mixture, then let it rest for 5 minutes.
4. Stir in flaxseed oil, cinnamon and nutmeg. Adjust the amount you like and serve.

Per serving: Calories: 133kcal; Fat: 4.6g; Carbs: 18.8g; Protein: 1.8g

14. Roasted Pears with Walnuts

Preparation time: 5 minutes

Cooking time: 25 minutes

Servings: 4

Ingredients:

- 4 Bosc or d'Anjou pears, cored and quartered, skin on
- ¼ cup low-fat blue cheese, crumbled
- ¼ cup toasted walnuts, coarsely chopped
- 1 tbsp. grape seed oil or canola
- 1 tbsp. lemon juice
- Cooking spray

Directions:

1. Preheat the oven to 425°F. Toss pears with oil and lemon juice in a medium bowl.
2. Spray the cooking spray on the baking sheet, and put pears, cut-side down, on it. Roast for 15 minutes. Flip pears and roast for 10 more minutes.
3. Remove from oven. Divide pears among four plates, and top each serving with 1 tbsp. cheese and nuts. Serve immediately.

Per serving: Calories: 200kcal; Fat: 11g; Carbs: 26.5g; Protein: 4.4g

15. Sweet Potatoes with Pineapple

Preparation time: 5 minutes

Cooking time: 10 minutes

Servings: 4

Ingredients:

- 2 tbsps. coconut oil or olive oil
- 1 cup pineapple chunks, drained
- 4 baked sweet potatoes, sliced

Directions:

1. Heat oil over medium-high in a huge nonstick pan and add sweet potatoes to the pan flesh-side down.
2. Cook for about 8 minutes, until the potatoes begin to brown and caramelize.
3. Put sweet potatoes on plates and top with pineapple. Serve.

Per serving: Calories: 233kcal; Fat: 7.2g; Carbs: 41.3g; Protein: 2.4g

16. Protein Packed Quinoa

Preparation time: 10 minutes

Cooking time: 15 minutes

Servings: 2

Ingredients:

- ½ cup quinoa, uncooked
- 1 tbsp peanut butter
- 1 ½ tbsp honey
- ½ tsp cinnamon
- 1 ¼ cup unsweetened almond milk

Directions:

1. Add quinoa and almond milk to a saucepan and bring to a boil.
2. Turn heat to low and simmer for 15 minutes or until quinoa is cooked.
3. Add honey and peanut butter and stir well. Turn off the heat.
4. Top with chopped nuts and serve.

Per serving: Calories: 271kcal; Fat: 9.3g; Carbs: 40.6g; Protein: 8.4g

17. Healthy Overnight Oatmeal

Preparation time: 5 minutes

Cooking time: 5 minutes

Servings: 1

Ingredients:

- ½ cup rolled oats
- 1 tbsp cashews, chopped
- 1 tbsp hazelnuts, chopped
- 1 tbsp honey
- ¼ cup unsweetened almond milk
- ½ tsp cinnamon
- ¼ cup pumpkin puree

Directions:

1. Mix oats, pumpkin puree, cinnamon, almond milk, and honey in a bowl.
2. Pour oats mixture into the mason glass jar and top with chopped hazelnuts and cashews.
3. Cover jar and place in refrigerator for overnight.
4. Serve and enjoy.

Per serving: Calories: 325kcal; Fat: 10.7g; Carbs: 51.6g; Protein: 8.9g

18. Delicious Breakfast Barley

Preparation time: 10 minutes

Cooking time: 30 minutes

Servings: 4

Ingredients:

- 1 cup pearl barley
- ¼ tsp ground cinnamon
- 2 tbsp hazelnuts, chopped
- 2 tbsp almonds, sliced
- ¼ cup frozen strawberries
- ¼ cup frozen blueberries
- 4 cups water
- Pinch of salt

Directions:

1. Add barley, water, and salt into a saucepan and bring to a boil.
2. Turn heat to low and simmer for 25-30 minutes or until the barley is cooked.
3. Remove saucepan from heat and allow to cool.
4. Add remaining ingredients and stir everything well.
5. Serve and enjoy.

Per serving: Calories: 237kcal; Fat: 4.4g; Carbs: 44.9g; Protein: 6.7g

19. Tasty Cherry Smoothie

Preparation time: 5 minutes

Cooking time: 5 minutes

Servings: 1

Ingredients:

- 1 cup cherries, seeded
- ¼ cup ice
- ¼ banana
- ½ cup strawberries
- 1 oz unsweetened dark chocolate, chopped
- 1 cup unsweetened fresh milk

Directions:

1. Bring all ingredients into the blender, then blend until smooth.
2. Serve immediately and enjoy.

Per serving: Calories: 372kcal; Fat: 19.2g; Carbs: 44.4g; Protein: 6.1g

20. Beet Berry Smoothie

Preparation time: 5 minutes

Cooking time: 5 minutes

Servings: 1

Ingredients:

- 1 small beet, peeled & chopped
- 1 cup unsweetened fresh milk
- ¼ avocado, scoop out the flesh
- ½ cup frozen strawberries

- ¼ cup frozen blueberries
- ¼ cup frozen raspberries

Directions:

1. Bring all ingredients into the blender and blend until smooth.
2. Serve immediately and enjoy.

Per serving: Calories: 290kcal; Fat: 13.7g; Carbs: 42.9g; Protein: 4.1g

21. Delicious Blueberry Smoothie

Preparation time: 5 minutes

Cooking time: 5 minutes

Servings: 2

Ingredients:

- 2 cups blueberries
- 1 ½ tbsp chia seeds
- 1 tsp vanilla
- ½ cup yogurt
- 1 avocado, scoop out the flesh
- ¼ tsp cinnamon
- 2 cups unsweetened fresh milk
- ½ lime juice

Directions:

1. Bring all ingredients into the blender and blend until smooth.
2. Serve immediately and enjoy.

Per serving: Calories: 386kcal; Fat: 24.8g; Carbs: 37.1g; Protein: 7.8g

CHAPTER 3: Sides

22. Okra and Tomato Casserole

Preparation time: 25 minutes

Cooking time: 26 minutes

Servings: 4

Ingredients:

- 1 lb. okra, trimmed
- 1 tomato, cut into wedges
- 1 garlic clove, chopped
- 1 cup fresh parsley leaves, finely cut
- 1 tbsp. extra virgin olive oil

Directions:

1. Preheat the oven to 350 degrees F.
2. In a deep ovenproof baking dish, combine okra, sliced tomatoes, olive oil and garlic.
3. Toss to combine and bake for 45 minutes. Drizzle with parsley and serve.

Per serving: Calories: 80kcal; Fat: 0.75g; Carbs: 16; Protein: 3g

23. Roasted Sweet Carrots

Preparation time: 2 minutes

Cooking time: 8 minutes

Servings: 4

Ingredients:

- 1 lb. sliced carrots
- ¼ tsp. white pepper
- 2 tbsps. lime juice
- 4 tbsps. honey
- ¼ tsp. salt

Directions:

1. Preheat the pan to a temperature of 350°F (180°C).
2. Add honey, salt, pepper, and lime juice to a bowl, then mix.
3. Now add the carrots and toss to combine.
4. Place the carrots in the fryer basket and cook for 8 minutes.

5. Serve!

Per serving: Calories: 69kcal; Fat: 0.25g; Carbs: 17g; Protein: 1.2g

24. Tomato and Avocado Salad

Preparation time: 10 minutes

Cooking time: 0 minute

Servings: 4

Ingredients:

- 1-pound of cherry tomatoes
- 2 avocados
- 1 sweet onion, chopped
- 2 tablespoons of lemon juice
- 1½ tablespoons of olive oil
- A handful of basil, chopped

Directions:

1. Mix the tomatoes with the avocados and the rest of the ingredients in a serving bowl, toss and serve right away!

Per serving: Calories: 168kcal; Fat: 11g; Carbs: 17g; Protein: 3.5g

25. Chickpea Salad

Preparation time: 15 minutes

Cooking time: 0 minute

Servings: 4

Ingredients:

- Cooked chickpeas (15 oz.)
- 1 diced Roma tomato
- ½ a green medium bell pepper, diced
- 1 tbsp of fresh parsley
- 1 small white onion
- ½ of minced garlic
- 1 lemon, juiced.

Directions:

1. Chop the tomato, green pepper, and onion.

2. Mince the garlic. Combine each of these in a salad bowl and toss well.
3. Cover the salad and chill for at least 15 minutes in the fridge.
4. Serve when ready.

Per serving: Calories: 152kcal; Fat: 2g; Carbs: 20g; Protein: 4g

26. Cauliflower Sprinkled with Curry

Preparation time: 10 minutes

Cooking time: 5 hours

Servings: 4

Ingredients:

- 1 cauliflower head, florets separated
- 2 carrots, sliced
- 1 red onion, chopped
- ¾ cup of coconut milk
- 2 garlic cloves, minced
- 2 tablespoons of curry powder
- A pinch of salt and black pepper
- 1 tablespoon of red pepper flakes
- 1 teaspoon of garam masala

Directions:

1. In your slow cooker, mix all of the ingredients.
2. Cover then cook on high for 5 hours
3. Divide into bowls and serve.

Per serving: Calories: 68kcal; Fat: 1.2g; Carbs: 13g; Protein: 3.5g

27. Roasted Broccoli Salad

Preparation time: 9 minutes

Cooking time: 17 minutes

Servings: 4

Ingredients:

- 1 lb. broccoli
- 3 tablespoons of olive oil
- 2 cups of cherry tomatoes
- 1 ½ teaspoon of honey
- 3 cups of whole grain bread, cubed

- 1 tablespoon of balsamic vinegar
- ½ teaspoon of black pepper
- ¼ teaspoon of sea salt, fine
- grated parmesan for serving

Directions:

1. Set the oven to 450 F, and then heat a rimmed baking sheet.
2. Drizzle your broccoli with a tablespoon of oil, and toss to coat.
3. Take out the baking sheet from the oven, and spoon the broccoli.
4. Put the remaining oil into the bottom of a bowl and add your tomatoes.
5. Toss them to coat, then mix tomatoes with a tablespoon of honey. Put on the baking sheet with the broccoli.
6. Roast for fifteen minutes, and stir halfway through your cooking time.
7. Add your bread and then roast for three more minutes.
8. Whisk two tablespoons of oil, vinegar, and the remaining honey. Season. Pour this over your broccoli mix to serve.

Per serving: Calories: 281kcal; Fat: 12g; Carbs: 38.5g; Protein: 8g

28. Chicken and Quinoa Salad

Preparation time: 10 minutes

Cooking time: 20 minutes

Servings: 2

Ingredients:

- 2 tablespoons of olive oil
- 2 ounces of quinoa
- 2 ounces of cherry tomatoes, cut in quarters
- 3 ounces of sweet corn
- Lime juice from 1 lime
- Lime zest from 1 lime, grated
- 2 spring onions, chopped
- A small red chili pepper, chopped
- 1 avocado

- 2 ounces of chicken meat

Directions:

1. Fill water in a pan and bring it to a boil over a medium-high heat
2. Add quinoa, stir and cook for 12 minutes.
3. Meanwhile, put the sweetcorn in a pan and heat over medium-high heat.
4. Cook for 5 minutes and leave aside for now.
5. Drain quinoa, transfer to a bowl and add tomatoes, corn, coriander, onions, chili, lime zest, olive oil, and salt and black pepper to taste and toss.
6. In another bowl, mix avocado with lime juice and stir well.
7. Add this to the quinoa salad and chicken.
8. Toss, coat, and serve.

Per serving: Calories: 300kcal; Fat: 16.5g; Carbs: 36g; Protein: 12.5g

29. Tofu with Brussels sprouts

Preparation time: 15 minutes

Cooking time: 15 minutes

Servings: 3

Ingredients:

- 5 tablespoons of olive oil
- 8 ounces of extra-firm tofu, drained, pressed, and cut into slices
- 2 garlic cloves, chopped
- 1/3 cup pecans, toasted and chopped
- 1 tablespoon unsweetened applesauce
- 1/4 cup fresh cilantro, chopped
- 1/2-pound Brussels sprouts, trimmed and cut into wide ribbons
- 3/4-pound mixed bell peppers, seeded and sliced

Directions:

1. In a skillet, heat a 1/2 tablespoon of the oil over medium heat and sauté the tofu for about 6–7 minutes, or until golden brown.

2. Add the garlic and pecans and sauté for about 1 minute.
3. Add the applesauce and cook for about 2 minutes.
4. Stir in the cilantro and remove from the heat.
5. Transfer the tofu onto a plate and set aside
6. Heat the remaining oil in the same skillet over medium-high heat and cook the Brussels sprouts and bell peppers for about 5 minutes.
7. Stir in the tofu and remove from the heat.
8. Serve immediately.

Per serving: Calories: 365kcal; Fat: 30g; Carbs: 11.5g; Protein: 11g

30. Avocado and Watermelon Mix

Preparation time: 10 minutes

Cooking time: 0 minutes

Servings: 4

Ingredients:

- 1½ cups of chopped tomatoes
- 1½ cups watermelon, cubed
- ½ jalapeno, chopped
- A pinch of salt and black pepper
- 1 avocado, peeled, pitted and cubed
- ½ teaspoon olive oil
- 2 tablespoons of ginger, grated
- Zest of 1 lime, grated
- 2 teaspoons of black sesame seeds
- 2 tablespoons of mint, chopped
- 3 tablespoons of lime juice

Directions:

1. In a salad bowl, combine the tomatoes with the watermelon, jalapeno, salt, pepper, avocado, oil, ginger, lime zest, black seeds, mint and lime juice.
2. Toss, divide between plates and serve as a side dish.

Per serving: Calories: 80kcal; Fat: 5g; Carbs: 8g; Protein: 2.2g

31. Celery and Chili Peppers Stir Fry

Preparation time: 10 minutes

Cooking time: 5 minutes

Servings: 6

Ingredients:

- 2 tablespoons of olive oil
- 3 chili peppers, dried and crushed
- 4 cups of julienned celery
- 2 tablespoons of coconut aminos

Directions:

1. Heat a pan with the oil at medium-high heat, add chili peppers, stir and cook them for 2 minutes.
2. Add the celery and the coconut aminos, stir and cook for 3 minutes.
3. Divide between plates and serve as a side dish.

Per serving: Calories: 42kcal; Fat: 2g; Carbs: 7.2g; Protein: 1.5g

32. Roasted Brussels sprouts

Preparation time: 5 minutes

Cooking time: 20 minutes

Servings: 4

Ingredients:

- 1½ pounds Brussels sprouts, trimmed and halved
- 2 tablespoons olive oil
- ¼ teaspoon salt
- ½ teaspoon freshly ground black pepper

Directions:

1. Preheat the oven to 400°f.
2. Combine the Brussels sprouts and olive oil in a large mixing bowl and toss until they are evenly coated.
3. Turn the Brussels sprouts onto a large baking sheet and flip them over, so they are cut-side down with the flat part touching the baking sheet. Sprinkle with salt and pepper.
4. Bake for 20-30 minutes or 'til the Brussels sprouts are lightly charred, crispy on the outside and toasted on the bottom. The outer leaves will be extra dark, too.
5. Serve immediately.

Per serving: Calories: 106kcal; Fat: 7g; Carbs: 11g; Protein: 4g

33. Sautéed Garlic Mushrooms

Preparation time: 10 minutes

Cooking time: 10 minutes

Servings: 4

Ingredients:

- 1 tablespoon of olive oil
- 3 cloves of garlic, minced
- 16 ounces of fresh brown mushrooms, sliced
- 7 ounces of fresh shiitake mushrooms, sliced
- ½ tsp of salt
- ½ tsp of pepper or more to taste

Directions:

1. Place a nonstick saucepan on medium-high heat and it for a minute.
2. Add oil and heat for 2 minutes.
3. Stir in the garlic and sauté for a minute.
4. Add the remaining ingredients and stir until soft and tender, for around 5 minutes.
5. Turn off the heat and let the mushrooms rest while the pan is covered for 5 minutes.
6. Serve and enjoy.

Per serving: Calories: 44kcal; Fat: 3.5g; Carbs: 2g; Protein: 2.2g

34. Cashew Pesto & Parsley With Veggies

Preparation time: 15 minutes

Cooking time: 10 minutes

Servings: 3-4

Ingredients:

- 3 zucchini (sliced)
- 8 bamboo skewers soaked in water
- 2 red capsicums
- ¼ cup olive oil
- 750 grams Eggplant
- 4 lemon wedges
- 1 cup of couscous salad
- Preparing the cashew pesto:
- ½ cup of cashew (roasted)
- ½ cup of parsley
- 2 cups of grated parmesan
- 2 tbsp of lime juice
- ¼ cup of olive oil

Directions:

1. Toss the capsicum, eggplant, and zucchini with oil and salt and thread them onto the skewers.
2. Cook the bamboo sticks for 6-8 minutes on a barbecue grill pan on medium heat.
3. Also, grill the lemon wedges on both sides.
4. To prepare the cashew pesto, combine all ingredients in the food processor and blend.
5. For serving, place the grill skewers on a plate with the grilled lemon slices and drizzle some cashew pesto over the top.

Per serving: Calories: 352kcal; Fat: 22g; Carbs: 20g; Protein: 25g

35. Turmeric Peppers Platter

Preparation time: 10 minutes

Cooking time: 20 minutes

Servings: 4

Ingredients:

- 2 green bell peppers, cut into wedges
- 2 red bell peppers, cut into wedges
- 2 yellow bell peppers, cut into wedges
- 2 tablespoons of avocado oil
- 2 garlic cloves, minced
- 1 bunch of basil, chopped
- A pinch of salt and black pepper
- 2 tablespoons of balsamic vinegar

Directions:

1. Heat a pan with the oil on medium heat, add the garlic and the vinegar and cook for 2 minutes.
2. Add the peppers and the other ingredients, toss, cook over medium heat for 18 minutes, arrange them on a platter and serve as an appetizer.

Per serving: Calories: 404kcal; Fat: 7.5g; Carbs: 9.5g; Protein: 1.75

36. Cabbage Sticks

Preparation time: 10 minutes

Cooking time: 30 minutes

Servings: 4

Ingredients:

- 1-pound cabbage leaves separated and cut into thick strips
- 1 tablespoon olive oil
- 1 tablespoon balsamic vinegar
- 1 teaspoon ginger, grated
- 1 teaspoon hot paprika
- A pinch of salt and black pepper

Directions:

1. Spread the cabbage strips on a baking sheet lined with parchment paper.
2. Add the oil, the vinegar, and the other ingredients, toss and cook at 400 degrees F for 30 minutes.
3. Divide the cabbage strips into bowls and serve as a snack.

Per serving: Calories: 75kcal; Fat: 3.5g; Carbs: 6.5g; Protein: 1.5g

CHAPTER 4: Vegetables

37. Sautéed Spinach with Pumpkin Seeds

Preparation time: 5 minutes

Cooking time: 15 minutes

Servings: 2

Ingredients:

- 2 tablespoons raw shelled pumpkin seeds
- 2 teaspoons extra-virgin olive oil
- 1 teaspoon balsamic vinegar
- 1 teaspoon water
- 1 bunch spinach, large stems removed
- 2 tablespoons crumbled goat cheese or feta cheese
- Freshly ground black pepper (optional)

Directions:

1. Preheat the oven to 350 deg. F.
2. Spread the pumpkin seeds on a rimmed baking sheet, and transfer them to the oven. Shake after 5 minutes, check after another 3 minutes, and take them out when they look golden and smell nutty, usually no more than 12 minutes total. Remove from the pan to cool.
3. Heat the oil, vinegar, and water in a large skillet over medium-high heat. When it is hot, add the spinach. Cover and cook for a minute, then stir, so the spinach gets coated with the oil and vinegar and barely wilts for another minute.
4. Transfer to a serving dish, and sprinkle with the toasted pumpkin seeds and goat cheese. Top with black pepper, if desired.

Per serving: Calories: 136kcal; Fat: 11g; Carbs: 5g; Protein: 7g

38. Spaghetti Squash with Walnuts and Parmesan

Preparation time: 5 minutes

Cooking time: 15 minutes

Servings: 4

Ingredients:

- 1 small spaghetti squash
- 2 tablespoons extra-virgin olive oil
- ¼ cup chopped walnuts, divided
- 1 garlic clove, minced
- ¼ cup grated Parmesan cheese, divided

Directions:

1. Poke the squash a few times with a fork, then microwave on high for 3 to 4 minutes to soften. Don't microwave for 5 minutes, or the steam buildup may cause it to burst.
2. Carefully halve the squash lengthwise. Use a spoon to scrape out the seeds. Place the halves, cut-sides down, in a microwave-safe baking dish. Pour in ½ inch of water.
3. Microwave on high until you can easily pierce the squash with a fork, 8 to 12 minutes.
4. Meanwhile, warm the oil, walnuts, and garlic in a small saucepan over low heat.
5. When the squash is done and cool enough to handle, use a fork to loosen the spaghetti-like strands of flesh. Pile them into four bowls, and top each with a quarter of the garlic-infused oil, walnuts, and cheese.

Per serving: Calories: 228kcal; Fat: 15g; Carbs: 24g; Protein: 5g

39. Sweet Spot Lentil Salad

Preparation time: 10 minutes

Cooking time: 0 minute

Servings: 3

Ingredients:

Dressing:

- 3 tablespoons apple cider vinegar
- 2 tablespoons extra-virgin olive oil
- 1 teaspoon water
- 1 teaspoon Dijon mustard
- ¼ teaspoon salt
- ¼ teaspoon freshly ground black pepper

Salad:

- 1 (15-ounce / 425-g) can of lentils, rinsed and drained
- 1 red bell pepper, seeded and chopped
- ½ cup frozen corn kernels, thawed
- ½ cup chopped snap peas
- ½ cup diced Jarlsberg cheese
- ¼ cup chopped fresh cilantro

Directions:

1. Whisk together the vinegar, oil, water, mustard, salt, and pepper in a huge bowl.
2. Add the lentils, bell pepper, corn, snap peas, cheese, and cilantro, and toss with the dressing.

Per serving: Calories: 440kcal; Fat: 17g; Carbs: 50g; Protein: 25g

40. Sesame Spinach

Preparation time: 10 minutes

Cooking time: 2 minutes

Servings: 3

Ingredients:

- ½ pound (227 g) spinach leaves
- 1 teaspoon minced garlic
- ½ tablespoon sesame oil
- Sea salt, to taste

- Freshly ground black pepper, to taste
- Sesame seeds

Directions:

1. Place a medium stockpot filled three-quarters full of water over high heat and bring to a boil.
2. Add the spinach and let boil for 1 to 2 minutes until softened.
3. Use a strainer to separate the spinach from the water and let it cool. Then use your hands to squeeze out as much liquid from the spinach as possible.
4. Cut the spinach into bite-size pieces and transfer it to a medium bowl.
5. Add the garlic and sesame oil and season with salt and pepper.
6. Sprinkle with sesame seeds and serve immediately.

Per serving: Calories: 56kcal; Fat: 4g; Carbs: 3g; Protein: 3g

41. Umami Mushrooms

Preparation time: 5 minutes

Cooking time: 15 minutes

Servings: 2

Ingredients:

- 8 ounces (227 g) white button, cremini, or portobello mushrooms
- 2 tablespoons extra-virgin olive oil
- 1 tablespoon balsamic vinegar
- 2 teaspoons reduced-sodium tamari
- 1 garlic clove, minced

Directions:

1. Rinse the mushrooms, then pat them dry with a paper towel. Trim them only if the ends look tough, and cut them into thick slices.
2. Preheat a heavy skillet over medium-high heat. Add the oil to the pan. When the oil is shimmering, add the mushrooms and toss to coat. Cook, stirring only occasionally, for

7 to 10 minutes until any water released by the mushrooms has evaporated, and they're golden brown. If they start to brown too quickly, turn down the heat.

3. Turn the heat down to medium-low. Add the balsamic vinegar and tamari, and sauté until dry. Add the garlic, then sauté for 1 minute.

Per serving: Calories: 157kcal; Fat: 14g; Carbs: 6g; Protein: 4g

42. Cauliflower Mashed "Potatoes"

Preparation time: 5 minutes
Cooking time: 8 minutes
Servings: 2
Ingredients:

- 1 (1½-pound / 680-g) head of cauliflower, chopped into florets
- 3 garlic cloves, chopped
- 1 teaspoon fresh thyme
- 1 teaspoon chopped fresh chives
- 1 teaspoon olive oil
- 2 tablespoons nonfat milk or plant-based milk
- Pinch salt to taste
- Pinch freshly ground black pepper

Directions:

1. Fill a huge saucepan with about 1 inch of water and insert a steamer basket. Bring the water to a boil and add the cauliflower florets to the basket. Decrease the heat to a simmer and cover, allowing the cauliflower to steam for 6 to 8 minutes or until fork-tender.

2. Drain the steamed cauliflower and transfer it to the bowl of a large food processor. Add the garlic, thyme, chives, olive oil, milk, salt, and pepper, and process to your desired texture. Serve warm.

Per serving: Calories: 119kcal; Fat: 3g; Carbs: 21g; Protein: 8g

43. Vegetable Kabobs

Preparation time: 25 minutes
Cooking time: 12 minutes
Servings: 2
Ingredients:

- 2 tablespoons olive oil
- 2 garlic cloves, crushed
- Juice of ½ lemon
- ½ teaspoon dried oregano
- ½ teaspoon dried basil
- Salt, to taste
- Freshly ground black pepper
- 1 cup cremini mushrooms
- ½ cup cherry tomatoes
- 1 green bell pepper, cut into chunks
- 1 red onion, cut into chunks
- 1 yellow squash, cut into thick rounds

Directions:

1. Preheat the oven to 400 deg. F.
2. Mix the olive oil, garlic, lemon juice, oregano, and basil in a bowl—season with salt and pepper.
3. Thread the mushrooms, tomatoes, bell pepper, onion, and squash onto skewers. Place the skewers on a baking sheet. Brush the vegetables with the oil mixture and let them sit for 10 to 15 minutes.
4. Roast for 10-12 minutes, or 'til tender, and serve immediately.

Per serving: Calories: 191kcal; Fat: 15g; Carbs: 15g; Protein: 4g

44. Perfect Sweet Potatoes

Preparation time: 5 minutes
Cooking time: 7 to 8 hours
Servings: 6
Ingredients:

- 6 sweet potatoes, washed and dried

Directions:

1. Loosely ball up 7 or 8 pieces of aluminum foil and place them in the bottom of a 6-quart slow cooker, covering about half the surface area.

2. Prick each sweet potato 6 to 8 times with a fork. Individually wrap each potato in a piece of foil and seal it completely. Place the wrapped sweet potatoes in the slow cooker on the foil balls.

3. Cover and cook on low for 7 to 8 hours. Use tongs to remove the sweet potatoes from the slow cooker. Allow the potatoes to cool slightly, then unwrap from the foil. Serve hot.

Per serving: Calories: 129kcal; Fat: 0g; Carbs: 30g; Protein: 2g

45. Almond Noodles with Cauliflower

Preparation time: 15 minutes

Cooking time: 20 minutes

Servings: 2

Ingredients:

- 8 oz.(230g) brown rice noodles
- 4 cups cauliflower florets (from about 2 large heads)
- ½ cup Greek yogurt
- 3 tbsps. almond butter
- 2 tbsps. apple cider
- 2 tbsps. low-sodium soy sauce
- 1 tbsp. ground fennel
- ½ tsp. crushed red pepper flakes

Directions:

1. Pour 6-8 cups of water into a medium pot and bring to a boil over medium-high heat. When boiling, add the rice noodles and cook following package instructions—usually 4 to 5 minutes, or until soft. Add the cauliflower florets to the cooking water and

cook for a further minute. Drain the noodles and cauliflower and set aside.

2. Mix the Greek yogurt, almond butter, apple cider, soy sauce, fennel, and crushed red pepper flakes in a large pot over low heat. Stir constantly and cook until smooth, 8 to 10 minutes.

3. Add the noodle and cauliflower mixture to the almond sauce. Use tongs to blend well.

Per serving: Calories: 299kcal; Fat: 5.28g; Carbs: 55.7g; Protein: 8.71g

46. Buckwheat with Potatoes and Kale

Preparation time: 15 minutes

Cooking time: 20 minutes

Servings: 4-6

Ingredients:

- 1 tbsp. coconut oil
- ½ cup buckwheat groats
- 2 cups cubed sweet potatoes
- 2 cups chopped kale, thoroughly washed and stemmed
- 1 yellow onion, chopped
- 2 garlic cloves, minced
- 2 tsps. ground cumin
- 1 cup lentils, rinsed
- 6 cups vegetable broth
- 1 tsp. salt
- ½ tsp. freshly ground black pepper

Directions:

1. Add the coconut oil to a large pot, and melt over medium-high heat. Stir in the sweet potatoes, onion, garlic, and cumin. Sauté for 5 minutes.

2. Stir in the buckwheat groats, lentils, vegetable broth, salt, and pepper. Bring to a boil. Lower the heat to simmer, and cover the pot. Cook until the sweet potatoes, buckwheat, and lentils are tender, about 15 minutes.

3. Take the pot off the heat. Stir in the kale to combine. Cover the pot and let it sit for 5 minutes; serve.

Per serving: Calories: 427kcal; Fat: 7g; Carbs: 69g; Protein: 24g

47. Easy Basic Table Salad

Preparation time: 5 minutes

Cooking time: 2 minutes

Servings: 2 bites

Ingredients:

- 1 head romaine lettuce coarsely chopped
- ½ cup sliced yellow onion (about ½ medium onion)
- ½–1 zucchini, cut in quarters
- 1 cup halved grape tomatoes
- ⅔ cup (160mL) almond butter
- 1 cup pressed and diced extra-firm tofu added in step 1
- 1 peach, pitted and diced
- Sprinkle of nutritional yeast
- toasted sesame

Directions:

1. Mix the lettuce, onion, zucchini, tofu, peach, nutritional yeast, sesame and tomatoes in a large bowl.
2. Top with the dressing, then toss to coat.

Per serving: Calories: 648kcal; Fat: 49.5g; Carbs: 42.4g; Protein: 21.8g

48. Grilled Cauliflower with Spicy Lentil Sauce

Preparation time: 15 minutes

Cooking time: 1.5 hours

Servings: 4

Ingredients:

- 2 medium heads of cauliflower
- 2 medium shallots, peeled and minced
- ½ cup green lentils, rinsed
- 2 cups (480 ml) low-sodium vegetable broth
- Chopped parsley
- 1 clove of garlic, peeled and minced
- ½ tsp. minced sage
- ½ tsp. ground fennel
- ½ tsp. crushed red pepper flakes
- Salt and freshly ground black pepper

Directions:

1. Cut each cauliflower head halfway through the vegetable stem, then trim each half, so you have a 1-inch-thick cutlet. Place each piece on a baking sheet. Save the extra cauliflower florets for other uses.
2. Put the shallots in a medium saucepan, then sauté over medium heat for 10 minutes. Add water 1 tbsp. at a time to keep the shallots from sticking to the pan. Add the garlic, fennel, sage, crushed red pepper flakes, and lentils and cook for 3 minutes. Add the vegetable stock and boil the mixture over high heat. Low the heat to medium and cook, covered, for 45 to 50 minutes. Add water as needed to keep the mix from drying out.
3. Puree the lentil mixture using an immersion blender. Return the puree to the pan if necessary and season with salt and pepper. Keep warm.
4. Prepare the grill.
5. Place the cauliflower on the grill, then cook each side for about 7 minutes.
6. Place the grilled cauliflower on a plate and spoon the sauce over them. Garnish with chopped parsley and serve.

Per serving: Calories: 79kcal; Fat: 1.03g; Carbs: 15.95g; Protein: 5.29g

49. Healthy Cauliflower Purée

Preparation time: 15 minutes

Cooking time: 10 minutes

Servings: 4

Ingredients:

- 1 garlic clove
- 1 head cauliflower, broken into florets
- ½ cup coconut milk
- 2 tsps. salt, divided
- ¼ tsp. freshly ground black pepper
- 1 tbsp. extra-virgin olive oil

Directions:

1. Boil a huge pot of water over high heat. After boiling, add cauliflower, garlic cloves and 1 tsp. of salt. Cook for about 5 minutes, until the cauliflower is soft.

2. Remove the cauliflower from the pot, drain it, and put it in a large bowl. Mash with a potato masher.

3. Sprinkle the remaining 1 tsp. of salt, pepper and coconut milk on the mashed cauliflower. Stir well.

4. Transfer the puree to a bowl and drizzle with olive oil.

Per serving: Calories: 117kcal; Fat: 11g; Carbs: 6g; Protein: 2g

50. Slow Cooker Quinoa Lentil Tacos

Preparation time: 5 minutes,

Cooking time: 10 hours (low), 5 hours (high)

Servings: 6

Ingredients:

- 1 tsp. smoked paprika
- 1 tbsp. Taco Seasoning Mix
- 1½ cups quinoa
- 1½ cup red lentils
- 6 cups of Vegetable Stock
- 2 tbsps. chopped chipotles in adobo, or more as desired
- Whole-wheat tortillas

Toppings:

- Chopped tomatoes
- Salsa

Directions:

1. Add all the taco ingredients except the tortillas and the toppings to the slow cooker.

2. Cover the cooker, then cook on low for 10 hours or high for 5 hours.

3. Place the tortillas in a dry skillet and warm over medium heat. Fill the warm tortillas with the filling and top with your chosen toppings. Fold in half to serve.

Per serving: Calories: 2387kcal; Fat: 229.5g; Carbs: 68.5g; Protein: 32.9g

51. Vegetable Fruit Bowl with Lentil

Preparation time: 20 minutes

Cooking time: 40 minutes

Servings: 4-6

Ingredients:

- 1 (15-ounce (425g)) can lentils, drained and rinsed
- 4 cups cooked brown rice
- 1 cup of red lentils
- 2 cups water
- Chicken Lettuce Wraps sauce
- 1 small jicama, peeled then cut into thin sticks, divided
- 1 head radicchio, cored and torn into pieces, divided
- 2 scallions, sliced, divided
- 2 red Bartlett (or other) ripe pears, cored, quartered, sliced, divided

Directions:

1. Mix the red lentils and water in a medium bowl. Put the lid on and put it in the refrigerator overnight. When you are ready to prepare the salad, remove the lentils and drain them.

2. Put the brown rice and canned lentils in a medium bowl and mix. Add half of the chicken lettuce wrap sauce. Let the mixture sit for at least 30 minutes or overnight.

3. Divide the lentil and rice mixture into several small bowls. Put an equal amount of drained red lentils in each bowl. Sprinkle with chicory, jicama, pear, and green onion separately for garnish.

4. Finally, top with some remaining chicken lettuce roll sauce and enjoy.

Per serving: Calories: 989kcal; Fat: 31g; Carbs: 151g; Protein: 31g

CHAPTER 5: Meat

52. Chicken Shaheata

Preparation time: 15 minutes

Cooking time: 30 minutes

Servings: 8

Ingredients:

- 2 lb. chicken breast, sliced into strips
- 1 teaspoon of paprika
- 1 teaspoon of ground cumin
- 1/4 teaspoon of garlic granules
- 1/2 teaspoon of turmeric
- 1/4 teaspoon of ground allspice

Directions:

1. Season, the chicken with the spices and a little salt and pepper.
2. Pour 1 cup of chicken broth into the pot.
3. Seal the pot.
4. Choose the poultry setting.
5. Cook for 15 minutes.
6. Release the pressure naturally.

Per serving: Calories: 146kcal; Fats 3.3g; Carbs: 2.6g; Protein: 26g

53. Amazing Grilled Chicken and Blueberry Salad

Preparation time: 10 minutes

Cooking time: 25 minutes

Servings: 5

Ingredients:

- 5 cups mixed greens
- 1 cup blueberries
- ¼ cup sliced almonds
- 2 cups chicken breasts, cooked and cubed
- For dressing
- ¼ cup olive oil
- ¼ cup apple cider vinegar
- ¼ cup blueberries

- 2 tablespoons honey
- Sunflower seeds and pepper to taste

Directions:

1. Mix well with greens, berries, almonds, and chicken cubes.
2. Take a bowl and mix the dressing ingredients; pour the mix into a blender and blitz until smooth.
3. Add dressing on top of the chicken cubes and toss well.
4. Season more, and enjoy!

Per serving: Calories: 126kcal; Fat: 4.6g; Carbs: 9g; Protein: 14g

54. Garlic Mushroom Chicken

Preparation time: 15 minutes

Cooking time: 15 minutes

Servings: 4

Ingredients:

- 4 chicken breasts, boneless and skinless
- 3 garlic cloves, minced
- 1 onion, chopped
- 2 cups mushrooms, sliced
- 1 tbsp olive oil
- ½ cup chicken stock
- ¼ tsp pepper
- ½ tsp salt

Directions:

1. Season the chicken with pepper and salt. Heat the oil in a pan on medium heat, then put the seasoned chicken in the pan and cook for 5-6 minutes on each side. Remove and place on a plate.
2. Add onion and mushrooms to the pan and sauté until tender, about 2-3 minutes. Add garlic and sauté for a minute. Add stock and bring to a boil. Stir well and cook for 1-2 minutes. Pour over the chicken and serve.

Per serving: Calories: 233kcal; Fat: 6g; Carbs: 4g; Protein: 21g

55. Hot Chicken Wings

Preparation time: 15 minutes

Cooking time: 25 minutes

Servings: 4

Ingredients:

- 10 - 20 chicken wings
- ½ stick of margarine
- 1 bottle of Durkee hot sauce
- 2 tablespoons of honey
- 10 shakes of Tabasco sauce
- 2 tablespoons of cayenne pepper

Directions:

1. Heat canola oil in a deep pot. Deep-fry the wings until cooked, approximately 20 minutes. Mix the hot sauce, honey, Tabasco, and cayenne pepper in a medium bowl. Mix well.

2. Place the cooked wings on paper towels. Drain the excess oil. Mix the chicken wings in the sauce until coated evenly.

Per serving: Calories: 475kcal; Fat: 34g; Carbs: 16g; Protein: 29g

56. Chicken Tikka

Preparation time: 15 minutes

Cooking time: 20 minutes

Servings: 6

Ingredients:

- 4 chicken breasts, skinless, boneless; cubed
- 2 large onions, cut into chunks
- 10 cherry tomatoes
- 1/3 cup plain non-fat yogurt
- 4 garlic cloves, crushed
- 1 ½" of fresh ginger, peeled and chopped
- 1 small onion, grated
- 1 ½ teaspoon chili powder
- 1 tablespoon of ground coriander
- 1 teaspoon of salt
- 2 tablespoons of coriander leaves

Directions:

1. In a large bowl, combine the non-fat yogurt, grated onion, crushed garlic, ginger, chili powder, coriander, salt, and pepper. Add the cubed chicken and stir until the chicken is coated.

2. Cover with plastic film and place in the fridge. Marinate for 2 – 4 hours.

3. Heat the broiler or barbecue.

4. After marinating the chicken, prepare some skewers—alternate pieces of chicken, cherry tomatoes and onion chunks onto the skewers.

5. Grill for 6 – 8 minutes on each side. Once the chicken is cooked, pull the meat and vegetables off the skewers and put them onto plates. Garnish with coriander. Serve immediately.

Per serving: Calories: 160kcal; Fat: 3.5g; Carbs: 8.3g; Protein: 11.5g

57. Meatballs

Preparation time: 10 minutes

Cooking time: 20 minutes

Servings: 8

Ingredients:

- 2 eggs
- 2 lbs. ground chicken
- 1 ½ tbsp garlic, minced
- 1 small onion, chopped
- ½ cup cilantro, chopped
- 8 oz goat cheese, crumbled
- 20 oz kale, frozen, thawed & squeezed
- ½ cup almond flour
- Pepper
- Salt

Directions:

1. Preheat the oven to 400 deg. F.

2. Add chicken and remaining ingredients into the large mixing bowl and mix until well combined.

3. Make a similar shape of balls from the chicken mixture and place them onto a parchment-lined baking sheet.

4. Bake in preheated oven for 15-20 minutes.

5. Serve and enjoy.

Per serving: Calories: 425kcal; Fat: 23.2g; Carbs: 6.4g; Protein: 46.7g

58. Tasty Chicken Wings

Preparation time: 10 minutes

Cooking time: 12 minutes

Servings: 15

Ingredients:

- 15 chicken wings
- ½ tsp coriander
- ½ tsp cumin powder
- ¼ tsp ground ginger
- ½ tsp turmeric
- 1 tbsp dried rosemary
- 1 ½ tsp smoked paprika
- 1 ½ tsp garlic powder
- 1 ½ tsp onion powder
- Pepper
- Salt

Directions:

1. Add chicken wings into the large mixing bowl.

2. Add remaining ingredients over chicken wings and mix until well coated.

3. Place chicken wings on preheated grill and cook for 8-12 minutes or until cooked.

4. Serve and enjoy.

Per serving: Calories: 281kcal; Fat: 10.9g; Carbs: 0.8g; Protein: 42.4g

59. Healthy Turkey Salad

Preparation time: 10 minutes

Cooking time: 5 minutes

Servings: 6

Ingredients:

- 20 oz cooked turkey breast, shredded
- ¼ cup feta cheese, crumbled
- ¼ cup almonds, sliced
- 2 tbsp pecans, chopped
- 2 tbsp walnuts, chopped
- ¼ cup dried cranberries, unsweetened
- 1 tbsp tarragon, chopped
- ¼ tsp Dijon mustard
- ½ cup light mayonnaise
- ¼ cup green onions, chopped
- 2 celery stalks, chopped
- Pepper
- Salt

Directions:

1. Add shredded turkey and remaining ingredients into the mixing bowl and mix until well combined.

2. Serve and enjoy.

Per serving: Calories: 269kcal; Fat: 16.4g; Carbs: 12g; Protein: 19.4g

60. Juicy Chicken Patties

Preparation time: 10 minutes

Cooking time: 10 minutes

Servings: 12

Ingredients:

- 1 lb. ground chicken
- 2 tbsp olive oil
- ¼ tsp red pepper flakes
- 1 scallion, chopped
- 1 egg yolk
- Pepper
- Salt

Directions:

1. In a mixing bowl, mix chicken, red pepper flakes, scallions, egg yolk, pepper, and salt until well combined.
2. Heat oil in a pan over medium-high heat.
3. Make small patties from the chicken mixture.
4. Place patties in hot oil and cook for 2-3 minutes on each side.
5. Serve and enjoy.

Per serving: Calories: 97kcal; Fat: 5.5g; Carbs: 0.2g; Protein: 11.2g

61. Spicy Chicken

Preparation time: 10 minutes
Cooking time: 18 minutes
Servings: 2
Ingredients:

- 2 chicken breasts, boneless
- 1 1/2 tsp chili powder
- 3 tbsp Sriracha sauce
- 1/4 tsp smoked paprika
- 2 tbsp sesame oil
- 1 tbsp brown sugar
- 1 tsp onion powder
- 1 tsp garlic powder
- Salt

Directions:

1. Preheat your air fryer to 350 F.
2. Add chicken and remaining ingredients into the large mixing bowl and mix until well coated.
3. Cover bowl and place in refrigerator for 6 hours.
4. Place marinated chicken into the air fryer basket and cook for 18 minutes. Turn halfway through.
5. Serve and enjoy.

Per serving: Calories: 433kcal; Fat: 25.3g; Carbs: 8g; Protein: 43g

62. Asian Chicken Breasts

Preparation time: 10 minutes
Cooking time: 10 minutes
Servings: 4
Ingredients:

- 1 lb. chicken breasts, boneless & skinless
- 1 1/2 tbsp fish sauce
- 1/2 cup unsweetened coconut milk
- 1 1/2 tbsp red curry paste
- 1 tsp brown sugar
- Pepper
- Salt

Directions:

1. Add chicken and remaining ingredients into the zip-lock bag.
2. Seal bag and place in refrigerator for 8 hours.
3. Place marinated chicken on a hot grill and cook for 10 minutes. Turn halfway through.
4. Serve and enjoy.

Per serving: Calories: 312kcal; Fat: 17.2g; Carbs: 3.8g; Protein: 33.8g

63. Delicious Chicken Tenders

Preparation time: 10 minutes
Cooking time: 10 minutes
Servings: 4
Ingredients:

- 1 1/2 lbs. chicken tenders
- 1 1/2 tbsp fresh rosemary, chopped
- 3 tbsp maple syrup
- 1/4 cup Dijon mustard
- 2 tbsp olive oil
- 1 tbsp lemon juice
- Pepper
- Salt

Directions:

1. Add chicken tenders and remaining ingredients into the zip-lock bag.

2. Seal bag and place in refrigerator for 6 hours.
3. Place marinated chicken tenders on a hot grill and cook for 10 minutes. Turn halfway through.
4. Serve and enjoy.

Per serving: Calories: 453kcal; Fat: 19.8g; Carbs: 14.7g; Protein: 49.4g

64. Italian Chicken Skewers

Preparation time: 10 minutes

Cooking time: 15 minutes

Servings: 6

Ingredients:

- 2 lbs. chicken breasts, boneless & cut into 1-inch pieces
- ½ tsp paprika
- 1 tbsp garlic, minced
- 2 tbsp lime juice
- ¼ cup olive oil
- 1 tsp rosemary, chopped
- 2 tsp dried oregano
- Pepper
- Salt

Directions:

1. Add chicken and remaining ingredients into the zip-lock bag.
2. Seal bag and place in refrigerator for 8 hours.
3. Thread marinated chicken onto the skewers and cook on a hot grill for 15 minutes. Turn halfway through.
4. Serve and enjoy.

Per serving: Calories: 368kcal; Fat: 19.7g; Carbs: 2.3g; Protein: 44g

65. Herb Chicken Breast

Preparation time: 10 minutes

Cooking time: 10 minutes

Servings: 4

Ingredients:

- 4 chicken breasts, boneless

For marinade:

- 1 tsp chili powder
- 1 tbsp garlic powder
- 1 lime zest
- 1/4 cup lime juice
- 1/4 cup olive oil
- 1/2 tsp smoked paprika
- 2 tsp oregano
- 2 tsp dried mixed herbs
- Pepper
- Salt

Directions:

1. Add chicken and remaining ingredients into the zip-lock bag.
2. Seal bag and place in refrigerator for overnight.
3. Place marinated chicken breasts on a hot grill and cook for 10 minutes. Turn halfway through.
4. Serve and enjoy.

Per serving: Calories: 417kcal; Fat: 23.8g; Carbs: 6.3g; Protein: 43.5g

66. Grill Lemon Chicken

Preparation time: 10 minutes

Cooking time: 10 minutes

Servings: 6

Ingredients:

- 2 lbs. chicken breasts, boneless
- 1 tbsp lemon zest
- 2 tbsp fresh lemon juice
- 3 tbsp olive oil
- 1 tsp chili powder
- 1 tsp paprika
- ¼ cup fresh cilantro, chopped

- 1 tsp ground coriander
- Pepper
- Salt

Directions:

1. Add chicken and remaining ingredients into the zip-lock bag.
2. Seal bag and place in refrigerator for 8 hours.
3. Place marinated chicken on a hot grill and cook for 10 minutes. Turn halfway through.
4. Serve and enjoy.

Per serving: Calories: 354kcal; Fat: 18.5g; Carbs: 1.1g; Protein: 44g

67. Creamy Chicken Salad

Preparation time: 10 minutes

Cooking time: 5 minutes

Servings: 6

Ingredients:

- 3 cups cooked chicken, shredded
- 1 ½ tbsp dill, chopped
- 2 tbsp apple cider vinegar
- ¼ cup yellow mustard
- 1 cup light mayonnaise
- 2 celery stalks, chopped
- 1 yellow onion, chopped
- 1 cup dill pickles, chopped
- Pepper
- Salt

Directions:

1. Add shredded chicken and remaining ingredients into the mixing bowl and mix until well combined.
2. Serve and enjoy.

Per serving: Calories: 280kcal; Fat: 15.7g; Carbs: 12.9g; Protein: 21.6g

68. Sweet & Tangy Chicken

Preparation time: 10 minutes

Cooking time: 6 hours

Servings: 6

Ingredients:

- 2 lbs. chicken breasts, boneless
- 1 tsp garlic, minced
- 6 tbsp maple syrup
- ¼ cup olive oil
- 1 ¼ tsp Worcestershire sauce
- ½ cup Dijon mustard
- Pepper
- Salts

Directions:

1. Place chicken into the slow cooker.
2. Mix the remaining ingredients and then pour over the chicken.
3. Cover then cook on low for 6 hours.
4. Shred the chicken using a fork and served.

Per serving: Calories: 439kcal; Fat: 20.4g; Carbs: 18.8g; Protein: 44.7g

69. Hearty Chicken Stew

Preparation time: 10 minutes

Cooking time: 6 hours

Servings: 6

Ingredients:

- 6 chicken thighs, boneless
- 2 cups chicken broth
- 1 ½ cups baby potatoes, cut in half
- 2 tomatoes, diced
- 1 tsp garlic, minced
- 1 small onion, diced
- 2 celery stalks, diced
- ¼ tsp chili powder
- 2 carrots, peeled& sliced
- Pepper
- Salt

Directions:

1. Place chicken into the slow cooker, then pour the remaining ingredients over the chicken.
2. Cover and then cook on low for 6 hours.
3. Shred chicken using a fork.
4. Stir well and serve.

Per serving: Calories: 308kcal; Fat: 11.1g; Carbs: 6.5g; Protein: 43.5g

70. Juicy Chicken Breast

Preparation time: 10 minutes

Cooking time: 6 hours

Servings: 4

Ingredients:

- 1 lb. chicken breasts, boneless
- ¼ cup chicken broth
- 1 tbsp garlic, minced
- 1 ½ tbsp brown sugar
- ¼ cup red wine vinegar

Directions:

1. Place chicken into the crockpot.
2. Pour the remaining ingredients over the chicken.
3. Cover and then cook on low for 6 hours.
4. Serve and enjoy.

Per serving: Calories: 235kcal; Fat: 8.5g; Carbs: 4.2g; Protein: 33g

71. Chicken with Orzo and Lemon

Preparation time: 10 minutes

Cooking time: 5 To 7 Hours on Low

Servings: 4

Ingredients:

- 3 cups low-sodium chicken broth
- 1 cup uncooked orzo pasta
- 1-pound boneless, skinless chicken breasts
- 1-pound carrots, peeled and diced
- 1 small onion, diced
- 3 celery stalks diced
- 2 garlic cloves, minced
- 1 teaspoon dried thyme
- 1 teaspoon ground turmeric
- ½ teaspoon salt
- ½ teaspoon freshly ground black pepper
- Juice of 1 lemon
- 2 dried bay leaves
- 2 tablespoons crumbled low-fat feta cheese (optional)

Directions:

1. The slow cooker combines broth, pasta, chicken, carrots, onion, celery, garlic, thyme, turmeric, salt, pepper, lemon juice, and bay leaves. Stir to mix well.
2. Cook on low for 5 to 7 hours.
3. Remove the bay leaves and top with the crumbled feta (if using) before serving.

Per serving: Calories: 288kcal; Fat: 13g; Carbs: 30g; Protein: 34g

CHAPTER 6: Seafoods

72. Mediterranean Baked Fish

Preparation time: 20 minutes
Cooking time: 45 minutes
Servings: 4
Ingredients:

- 2 teaspoons olive oil
- 1 large onion, sliced
- 1 can (16-ounce / 454-g) whole tomatoes, drained (reserve juice), and coarsely chopped
- 1 cup dry white wine
- ½ cup tomato juice (reserved from canned tomatoes)
- ¼ cup lemon juice
- ¼ cup orange juice
- 1 clove of garlic, minced
- 1 tablespoon fresh orange peel, grated
- 1 teaspoon fennel seeds, crushed
- ½ teaspoon dried oregano, crushed
- ½ teaspoon dried thyme, crushed
- ½ teaspoon dried basil, crushed
- 1 bay leaf
- Black pepper, to taste
- 1-pound (454 g) fish fillets (sole, flounder, or sea perch)

Directions:

1. Heat oil in a large nonstick skillet. Add onion and sauté over moderate heat for 5 minutes or until soft.
2. Add all remaining ingredients except fish. Stir well and simmer uncovered for 30 minutes.
3. Arrange fish in a 10- by 6-inch baking dish. Cover with sauce. Bake uncovered at 375 deg. F (190ºC) for about 15 minutes or until fish flakes easily.

Per serving: Calories: 178kcal; Fat: 4g; Carbs: 12g; Protein: 22g

73. Rosemary-Lemon Salmon

Preparation time: 5 minutes
Cooking time: 15 minutes
Servings: 4
Ingredients:

- 1 pound (454 g) sustainably sourced fresh, skin-on salmon fillets
- Zest and juice of ½ lemon (about 1½ tablespoons juice)
- 1 garlic clove, minced
- ¼ teaspoon kosher salt
- Freshly ground black pepper, to taste
- 2 fresh rosemary sprigs or 1 teaspoon dried rosemary
- 1 tablespoon extra-virgin olive oil (optional)

Directions:

1. Set the oven rack to the second-highest level, and preheat the broiler.
2. Line a rimmed baking sheet with aluminum foil. Bring the salmon, skin-side down, on the sheet. Top with the lemon zest and juice, garlic, salt, and pepper. Lay the rosemary sprigs on top. Drizzle with olive oil (if using).
3. Broil the salmon for 5 minutes, then move to a lower rack and reduce the heat to 325 deg. F (165ºC).
4. Cook for another 8-10 minutes until the salmon is nearly done. Let the fish rest, tented with foil, for 5 minutes before serving.

Per serving: Calories: 193kcal; Fat: 11g; Carbs: 1g; Protein: 23g

74. Crispy Trout with Herb

Preparation time: 10 minutes

Cooking time: 20 minutes

Servings: 2

Ingredients:

- 1 lb. (454 g) fresh trout (2 pieces)
- 2 cups (480 ml) fish stock
- ¼ tsp. dried thyme, ground
- 1 tbsp. fresh parsley, chopped
- 1 tbsp. fresh mint, chopped
- 3 tbsps. olive oil
- 2 tbsps. fresh lemon juice
- 3 garlic cloves, chopped
- 1 tsp. sea salt

Directions:

1. Mix mint, parsley, thyme, garlic, lemon juice, olive oil, and salt in a bowl. Stir to combine. Spread the fish and brush with the marinade. Set aside.
2. Insert the trivet into the instant pot. Pour in the stock and put the fish on top. Seal the lid and cook on Steam mode for 15 minutes with High Pressure. Quick release and serve immediately.

Per serving: Calories: 729kcal; Fat: 45.46g; Carbs: 3.66g; Protein: 72.49g

75. Grilled Halibut and Fruit Salsa

Preparation time: 20 minutes (includes marinating time)

Cooking time: 5 minutes

Servings: 4

Ingredients:

For the salsa

- 2 jalapeños, seeded and minced
- 1 garlic clove, minced
- 1⅓ cups diced papaya or mango (about 1 pound, 454 g)
- 1 red bell pepper, diced

- ⅓ cup thinly sliced scallions
- ¼ cup lime juice
- 2 tbsps. chopped cilantro

For the fish

- ½ tsp. paprika
- 1 garlic clove, minced
- ½ tsp. freshly ground pepper
- four 6-ounce (170 g) skinless halibut fillets
- 1 tbsp. lemon juice
- 1 tbsp. olive oil
- cooking spray

Directions:

For the salsa:

1. Put all the ingredients in a medium bowl and stir to combine.

For the fish:

2. In a large baking dish, stir the olive oil, garlic, lemon juice, paprika, and pepper. Add the fish to the mixture, turn to coat, and let stand for 10 minutes.
3. Spray a grill pan with cooking spray and heat to medium-high heat.
4. Remove the fish from the marinade, discard the marinade, and place it on the hot grill pan. Cook for about 3 minutes per side, or until the desired degree of doneness is reached. Serve topped with salsa.

Per serving: Calories: 169kcal; Fat: 9.9g; Carbs: 14.45g; Protein: 7.55g

76. Salmon Wrap

Preparation time: 15 minutes

Cooking time: 0 minutes

Servings: 1

Ingredients:

- 2 oz. low-salt Smoked Salmon
- 2 teaspoon low-fat cream cheese
- ½ medium-size red onion, finely sliced
- ½ teaspoon fresh basil or dried basil
- Pinch of pepper

- Arugula leaves, ½ cup
- 1 Homemade wrap or any whole-meal tortilla

Directions:

1. Heat the wrap or tortilla in a heated pan or oven. Combine cream cheese, basil, and pepper, and spread on the tortilla. Top with salmon, arugula, and sliced onion. Roll up and slice. Serve and enjoy!

Per serving: Calories: 285kcal; Fat: 12g; Carbs: 30g; Protein: 20g

77. Flounder with Tomatoes and Basil

Preparation time: 15 minutes

Cooking time: 20 minutes

Servings: 4

Ingredients:

- 1-pound cherry tomatoes
- 4 garlic cloves, sliced
- 2 tablespoons extra-virgin olive oil
- 2 tablespoons lemon juice
- 2 tablespoons basil, cut into ribbons
- ½ teaspoon kosher salt
- ¼ teaspoon freshly ground black pepper
- 4 (5- to 6-ounce) flounder fillets

Directions:

1. Preheat the oven to 425°F.
2. Mix the tomatoes, garlic, olive oil, lemon juice, basil, salt, and black pepper in a baking dish—Bake for 5 minutes.
3. Remove, then arrange the flounder on top of the tomato mixture. Bake until the fish is opaque and begins to flake, depending on thickness, for about 10 to 15 minutes.

Per serving: Calories: 73kcal; Fat: 4g; Carbs: 5g; Protein: 7g

78. Sardine Bruschetta with Fennel and Lemon Crema

Preparation time: 15 minutes

Cooking time: 0 minutes

Servings: 4

Ingredients:

- 1/3 cup plain Greek yogurt
- 2 tablespoons mayonnaise
- 2 tablespoons lemon juice
- 2 teaspoons lemon zest
- A pinch of salt
- 1 fennel bulb, cored and thinly sliced
- ¼ cup parsley, chopped, plus more for garnish
- ¼ cup of fresh mint, chopped
- 2 teaspoons extra-virgin olive oil
- 1/8 teaspoon freshly ground black pepper
- 8 slices of multigrain bread, toasted
- 2 (4.4-ounce) cans of smoked sardines

Directions:

1. Mix the yogurt, mayonnaise, 1 tablespoon lemon juice, lemon zest, and ¼ teaspoon salt in a small bowl.
2. Mix the remaining ½ teaspoon of salt, 1 tablespoon of lemon juice, the fennel, parsley, mint, olive oil, and black pepper in a separate small bowl.
3. Spoon 1 tablespoon of the yogurt mixture on each piece of toast. Divide the fennel mixture evenly on top of the yogurt mixture. Divide the sardines between the toasts, placing them on top of the fennel mixture. Garnish with more herbs, if desired.

Per serving: Calories: 241kcal; Fat: 8g; Carbs: 25g; Protein: 17g

79. Chopped Tuna Salad

Preparation time: 15 minutes

Cooking time: 0 minutes

Servings: 4

Ingredients:

- 2 tablespoons extra-virgin olive oil
- 2 tablespoons lemon juice
- 2 teaspoons Dijon mustard

- ¼ teaspoon freshly ground black pepper
- 12 olives, pitted and chopped
- ½ cup celery, diced
- ½ cup red onion, diced
- ½ cup red bell pepper, diced
- ½ cup fresh parsley, chopped
- 2 (6-ounce) cans of no-salt-added tuna packed in water, drained
- 6 cups of baby spinach

Directions:

1. Mix the olive oil, lemon juice, mustard, and black pepper in a medium bowl.
2. Add in the olives, celery, onion, bell pepper, and parsley and mix well.
3. Add the tuna and gently incorporate.
4. Divide the spinach evenly between 4 plates or bowls.
5. Spoon the tuna salad evenly on top of the spinach.

Per serving: Calories: 146kcal; Fat: 11g; Carbs: 5g; Protein: 9g

80. Green Goddess Crab Salad with Endive

Preparation time: 15 minutes

Cooking time: 10 minutes

Servings: 4

Ingredients:

- ½ pound lump crabmeat
- 2/3 cup plain Greek yogurt
- 3 tablespoons mayonnaise
- 3 tablespoons fresh chives, chopped, plus extra for garnish
- 3 tablespoons fresh parsley, chopped, plus extra for garnish
- 3 tablespoons fresh basil, chopped, plus extra for garnish
- Zest of 1 lemon
- Juice of 1 lemon

- ¼ teaspoon freshly ground black pepper
- 4 endives, ends cut off and leaves separated

Directions:

1. In a medium bowl, combine the crab, yogurt, mayonnaise, chives, parsley, basil, lemon zest, lemon juice, salt, and black pepper until well combined.
2. Place the endive leaves on 4 salad plates. Divide the crab mixture evenly on top of the endive. Garnish with additional herbs, if desired.

Per serving: Calories: 154kcal; Fat: 4g; Carbs: 5g; Protein: 22g

81. Lemon Salmon with Kaffir Lime

Preparation time: 15 minutes

Cooking time: 30 minutes

Servings: 1

Ingredients:

- A whole side of salmon fillet
- 1 thinly sliced lemon
- 2 kaffir torn lime leaves
- 1 quartered and bruised lemongrass stalk
- 1 ½ cups fresh coriander leaves

Directions:

1. Heat oven to 350 F. Covers a baking pan with foil sheets, overlapping the sides (enough to fold over the fish).
2. Put the salmon on the foil, and top with the lemon, lime leaves, lemongrass, and 1 cup of coriander leaves. Option: season with salt and pepper.
3. Bring the long side of the foil to the center before folding to seal. Roll the ends to wrap up the salmon—Bake for 30 minutes. Transfer the cooked fish to a platter. Top with fresh coriander. Serve with white or brown rice.

Per serving: Calories: 276kcal; Fat: 17g; Carbs: 12g; Protein: 24g

82. Baked Fish Served with Vegetables

Preparation time: 15 minutes
Cooking time: 30 minutes
Servings: 4
Ingredients:

- 4 haddock or cod fillets, skinless
- 2 Zucchinis, sliced into thick pieces
- 2 red onions, sliced into thick pieces
- 3 large tomatoes, cut into wedges
- ¼ cup black olives pitted
- ¼ cup flavorless oil (olive, canola, or sunflower)
- 1 tablespoon lemon juice
- 1 tablespoon Dijon mustard
- 2 garlic cloves, minced
- ½ cup chopped parsley

Directions:

1. Heat oven to 400 F. In a large baking dish, drizzle some oil over the bottom. Place the fish in the middle. Surround the fish with zucchini, tomato, onion, and olives. Drizzle more oil over the vegetables and fish— season with salt and pepper.

2. Place the baking dish in the oven. Bake for 30 minutes until the fish is flaky and the vegetables are tender. Whisk the lemon juice, garlic, mustard, and remaining oil in another bowl. Set aside.

3. Split the cooked vegetables between plates, then top with the fish. Drizzle the dressing over the vegetables and fish. Garnish with parsley.

Per serving: Calories: 195kcal; Fat: 6g; Carbs:14g; Protein: 23g

83. Spicy Cod

Preparation time: 15 minutes
Cooking time: 30 minutes
Servings: 4
Ingredients:

- 1-pound cod fillets
- 1 tablespoon flavorless oil (olive, canola, or sunflower)
- 1 cup low sodium salsa
- 2 tablespoons fresh chopped parsley

Directions:

1. Heat oven to 350 F. Drizzle the oil along the bottom of a large, deep baking dish. Place the cod fillets in the container. Pour the salsa over the fish.

2. Cover with foil for 20 minutes. Remove the foil for the last 10 minutes of cooking. Bake in the oven for 20 – 30 minutes, until the fish is flaky. Serve with white or brown rice. Garnish with parsley.

Per serving: Calories: 135kcal; Fat: 4.5g; Carbs: 2.5g; Protein: 20g

84. Easy Shrimp

Preparation time: 15 minutes
Cooking time: 10 minutes
Servings: 4
Ingredients:

- 1-pound cooked shrimp
- 1 pack of mixed frozen vegetables (0,5 oz)
- 1 garlic clove, minced
- 1 teaspoon butter or margarine
- ¼ cup of water
- 1 pack of shrimp-flavoured instant noodles
- ½ teaspoon ground ginger

Directions:

1. In a large skillet, melt the butter. Add the minced garlic and sweat it for 1 minute. Add the shrimp and vegetables to the skillet—

season with salt and pepper. Cover and simmer for 5 - 10 minutes, until the shrimp turns pink and the vegetables are tender.

2. Boil water in a separate pot. Add the noodles. Turn off the heat, and cover the pot. Let it stand for 3 minutes. (Retain the water.)

3. Transfer the noodles to the skillet with the shrimp and vegetables using a scoop or tongs. Stir in the seasoning packet. Mix, then serve immediately.

Per serving: Calories: 198kcal; Fat: 4g; Carbs: 11g; Protein: 30g

85. Ginger Sesame Salmon

Preparation time: 15 minutes

Cooking time: 5 minutes

Servings: 2

Ingredients:

- 4 ounces salmon
- 1/8 cup low-sodium soy sauce
- 2 tablespoons of balsamic vinegar
- ½ teaspoon sesame oil
- 2-inch chunk ginger, peeled and grated
- 1 garlic clove, minced
- 1 teaspoon flavorless oil (olive, canola, or sunflower)
- 1 teaspoon sesame seeds
- 1 teaspoon green onion, minced

Directions:

1. Combine the soy sauce, balsamic vinegar, sesame oil, garlic, and ginger in a glass dish. Place the salmon in the container. Cover and marinate for 15 - 60 minutes in the fridge.

2. In a nonstick skillet, heat 1 teaspoon of oil. Sauté the fish until it becomes firm and golden on each side. Sprinkle the sesame seeds in the pan—heat for 1 minute. Serve immediately. Garnish with green onion.

Per serving: Calories: 218kcal; Fat: 13.5g; Carbs: 6.5g; Protein: 17g

86. Steamed Veggie and Lemon Pepper Salmon

Preparation time: 15 minutes

Cooking time: 15 minutes

Servings: 4

Ingredients:

- 1 carrot, peeled and julienned
- 1 red bell pepper, julienned
- 1 zucchini, julienned
- ½ lemon, sliced thinly
- 1 tsp pepper
- ½ tsp salt
- 1/2-lb salmon filet with skin on
- A dash of tarragon

Directions:

1. Add salmon skin side down in a heat-proof dish that fits inside a saucepan—season with pepper. Add slices of lemon on top.

2. Place the julienned vegetables on top of the salmon and season with tarragon. Cover the top of the fish with the remaining cherry tomatoes and place the dish on the trivet. Cover the dish with foil. Cover the pan and steam for 15 minutes. Serve and enjoy.

Per serving: Calories: 125kcal; Fat: 3g; Carbs: 7g; Protein: 17g

87. Garlic and Tomatoes on Mussels

Preparation time: 15 minutes

Cooking time: 15 minutes

Servings: 6

Ingredients:

- ¼ cup white wine
- ½ cup of water
- 3 Roma tomatoes, chopped
- 2 cloves of garlic, minced
- 1 bay leaf

- 1 pound of mussels, scrubbed
- ½ cup fresh parsley, chopped
- 1 tbsp oil
- Pepper

Directions:

1. Heat a pot on medium-high heat for 3 minutes. Add oil and stir around to coat the pot with oil. Sauté the garlic, bay leaf, and tomatoes for 5 minutes.
2. Add the remaining ingredients except for parsley and mussels. Mix well. Add mussels. Cover, and boil for 5 minutes. Serve with a sprinkle of parsley and discard any unopened mussels.

Per serving: Calories: 100kcal; Fat: 3g; Carbs: 3g; Protein: 4.6g

88. Creamy Haddock with Kale

Preparation time: 15 minutes
Cooking time: 10 minutes
Servings: 5
Ingredients:

- 1 tbsp olive oil
- 1 onion, chopped
- 2 cloves of garlic, minced
- 2 cups of chicken broth
- 1 teaspoon of crushed red pepper flakes
- 1-pound wild Haddock fillets
- 3 tbsp thick cream
- 1 tablespoon basil
- 1 cup kale leaves, chopped
- Pepper to taste

Directions:

1. Place a pot on medium-high heat for 3 minutes. Add oil, then sauté the onion and garlic for 5 minutes.
2. Add the rest of the ingredients, excluding the basil, and mix well. Simmer on low heat for 5 minutes. Serve with a sprinkle of basil.

Per serving: Calories: 183kcal; Fat: 12g; Carbs: 4g; Protein: 15g

89. Coconut Curry Sea Bass

Preparation time: 15 minutes
Cooking time: 15 minutes
Servings: 3
Ingredients:

- 1 can of coconut milk
- Juice of 1 lime, freshly squeezed
- 1 tablespoon red curry paste
- 1 teaspoon coconut aminos
- 1 teaspoon of honey
- 2 teaspoons sriracha
- 2 cloves of garlic, minced
- 1 teaspoon ground turmeric
- 1 tablespoon curry powder
- ¼ cup fresh cilantro
- Pepper

Directions:

1. Place a heavy-bottomed pot on medium-high heat. Mix in all the ingredients, then simmer on low heat for 5 minutes. Serve and enjoy.

Per serving: Calories: 55kcal; Fat: 3g; Carbs: 7g; Protein: 1g

90. Stewed Cod Filet with Tomatoes

Preparation time: 15 minutes
Cooking time: 15 minutes
Servings: 6
Ingredients:

- 1 tbsp olive oil
- 1 onion, sliced
- 1 ½ pound fresh cod filets
- Pepper
- 1 lemon juice, freshly squeezed
- 1 can of diced tomatoes

Directions:

1. Sauté the onion for 2 minutes in a pot on medium-high heat.
2. Stir in diced tomatoes and cook for 5 minutes.
3. Add the cod filet and season with pepper.
4. Simmer on low heat for 5 minutes. Serve with freshly squeezed lemon juice.

Per serving: Calories: 93kcal; Fat: 2.5g; Carbs: 3.5g; Protein: 14.5g

91. Spicy Shrimp

Preparation time: 10 minutes

Cooking time: 6 minutes

Servings: 8

Ingredients:

- 1 lb. shrimp, peeled & deveined
- For marinade:
- 1 lime juice
- 2 garlic cloves, minced
- 3 tbsp Sriracha sauce
- 1/2 cup orange juice
- 1/4 cup olive oil
- Pepper
- Salt

Directions:

1. Add shrimp and remaining ingredients into the mixing bowl and mix well.
2. Cover and place in the refrigerator for 30 minutes.
3. Thread marinated shrimp onto the skewers.
4. Arrange skewers onto a hot grill and cook for 6 minutes. Turn halfway through.
5. Serve and enjoy.

Per serving: Calories: 132kcal; Fat: 7.4g; Carbs: 2.9g; Protein: 13.2g

CHAPTER 7: Soups

92. Healthy Bean Soup

Preparation time: 10 minutes

Cooking time: 6 hours

Servings: 6

Ingredients:

- 1 lb. dried great northern beans, soak overnight & drained
- 2 cups water
- 4 cups vegetable broth
- ½ tsp dried sage
- 1 tbsp garlic, minced
- 1 yellow onion, diced
- 2 celery stalks, diced
- 2 large carrots, diced
- Pepper
- Salt

Directions:

1. Add beans and remaining ingredients into the slow cooker and stir well.
2. Cover and then cook on high for 6 hours.
3. Stir well and serve.

Per serving: Calories: 281kcal; Fat: 1g; Carbs: 52.5g; Protein: 17.3g

93. Flavors Corn Soup

Preparation time: 10 minutes

Cooking time: 8 hours

Servings: 8

Ingredients:

- 20 oz can corn, drained
- 3 cups vegetable broth
- 1/2 tsp coriander powder
- ½ tsp thyme
- 1 tsp cumin powder
- 1 ½ jalapeno pepper, seeded & chopped
- 2 large potatoes, cut into chunks
- Pepper
- Salt

Directions:

1. Add corn and remaining ingredients into the slow cooker and stir everything well.
2. Cover and cook on low for 8 hours.
3. Stir well and serve.

Per serving: Calories: 125kcal; Fat: 0.9g; Carbs: 28.5g; Protein: 3.7g

94. Healthy Mushroom Soup

Preparation time: 10 minutes

Cooking time: 5 minutes

Servings: 1

Ingredients:

- ¼ cup mushrooms, chopped
- ½ cup unsweetened almond milk
- ¾ cup vegetable broth
- 2 tbsp olive oil
- 3 tbsp rice flour
- Pepper
- Salt

Directions:

1. Heat oil into the saucepan over medium heat.
2. Add mushrooms and sauté until softened.
3. Add flour and cook for a minute. Add broth and milk and stir well.
4. Turn heat to low and simmer until thickened. Season with pepper and salt.
5. Stir well and serve.

Per serving: Calories: 377kcal; Fat: 30.3g; Carbs: 26.1g; Protein: 3.1g

95. Potato Squash Soup

Preparation time: 10 minutes

Cooking time: 22 minutes

Servings: 4

Ingredients:

- 2 large summer squash, cut into half
- 2 tbsp fresh lemon juice
- ½ cup unsweetened coconut milk
- 4 cups vegetable broth
- 1 tbsp olive oil
- 1 tsp garlic, minced
- 1 potato, peeled & diced
- 1 yellow onion, diced
- Pepper
- Salt

Directions:

1. Heat oil into the pot over medium heat.
2. Add all veggies and sauté for 5 minutes.
3. Add broth and stir well, and bring to boil.
4. Turn heat to low and simmer vegetables for 15-20 minutes. Remove from heat.
5. Puree the soup using a blender until smooth.
6. Stir in lemon juice and coconut milk. Season with pepper and salt.
7. Serve and enjoy.

Per serving: Calories: 200kcal; Fat: 12.3g; Carbs: 17.1g; Protein: 7.5g

96. Silky Zucchini Soup

Preparation time: 10 minutes

Cooking time: 30 minutes

Servings: 4

Ingredients:

- 6 cups zucchini, chopped
- 1 ½ cups vegetable broth
- 1 tbsp olive oil
- 1 tbsp garlic, minced
- 1 medium onion, chopped
- ¼ tsp chili powder
- Pepper
- Salt

Directions:

1. Heat oil into the pot over medium heat.
2. Add onion and sauté for 5 minutes.
3. Add garlic and sauté for a minute.
4. Add zucchini, chili powder, pepper, and salt, and sauté for 10 minutes.
5. Add broth and stir well, reduce heat and simmer for 15 minutes.
6. Puree the soup using a blender until smooth.
7. Serve and enjoy.

Per serving: Calories: 74kcal; Fat: 3.9g; Carbs: 9.4g; Protein: 2.7g

97. Flavors Vegetable Stew

Preparation time: 10 minutes

Cooking time: 8 hours

Servings: 6

Ingredients:

- 1 cup frozen peas
- 1 cup frozen corn
- 2 lbs. potatoes, peeled & cubed
- 4 large carrots, peeled & diced
- 1 medium onion, chopped
- ½ cup unsweetened coconut milk
- ½ tsp dried oregano
- 1 tsp garlic powder
- 4 cups vegetable broth
- Pepper
- Salt

Directions:

1. Add all ingredients except coconut milk into the slow cooker and stir well.
2. Cover and cook on low for 8 hours.
3. Stir in coconut milk and serve.

Per serving: Calories: 226kcal; Fat: 5.4g; Carbs: 40.9g; Protein: 6.2g

98. Lentil Veggie Stew

Preparation time: 10 minutes

Cooking time: 4 hours

Servings: 8

Ingredients:

- 1 cup green lentils, rinsed
- ¼ cup olive oil
- ¼ tsp chili powder
- ½ tsp dried thyme
- ½ tsp dried oregano
- ½ cup wheat berries
- 4 cups vegetable broth
- 1 tsp garlic, minced
- 2 potatoes, peeled & diced
- 3 carrots, peeled & diced
- 2 celery stalks, sliced
- 1 medium onion, chopped
- Pepper
- Salt

Directions:

1. Add green lentils and remaining ingredients into the slow cooker and stir well.
2. Cover and then cook on high for 4 hours.
3. Stir well and serve.

Per serving: Calories: 209kcal; Fat: 6.8g; Carbs: 30g; Protein: 8.2g

99. Tuscan Fish Stew

Preparation time: 10 minutes

Cooking time: 20 minutes

Servings: 4

Ingredients:

- 1 tablespoon olive oil
- 1 onion, chopped
- 2 cloves garlic, minced
- 3 large tomatoes, chopped
- 1 bulb fennel, peeled, chopped, and rinsed
- 1 (14-ounce/397-g) can of artichoke hearts, drained
- 1 bay leaf
- ⅛ teaspoon red pepper flakes
- 2 cups low-sodium vegetable broth
- ¾ pound (340 g) halibut fillets, cubed
- ¼ pound (113 g) of sea scallops
- 1 slice low-sodium whole-wheat bread, crumbled
- 2 tablespoons chopped fresh basil
- 2 teaspoons chopped fresh oregano
- 2 tablespoons chopped fresh flat-leaf parsley

Directions:

1. Heat the olive oil over medium heat in a stockpot or huge saucepan.
2. Add the onion and garlic, and then cook while stirring for 3 minutes.
3. Add the tomatoes, fennel, artichoke hearts, bay leaf, red pepper flakes, and vegetable broth, and bring to a simmer. Simmer for 5 minutes.
4. Add the halibut fillets, and simmer for 4 minutes. Then add the scallops, and simmer for 3 minutes, or until the fillets flake when tested with a fork and the scallops are opaque.
5. Stir in the bread crumbs, then cover the pan and remove from the heat. Let it stand for 3 minutes.
6. Remove and discard the bay leaf. Top the soup with the fresh basil, oregano, and parsley, and serve.

Per serving: Calories: 210kcal; Fat: 6g; Carbs: 28g; Protein: 29g

100. Thick & Creamy Potato Soup

Preparation time: 10 minutes

Cooking time: 6 hours

Servings: 6

Ingredients:

- 6 cups sweet potatoes, diced
- ¼ tsp cinnamon
- ¼ tsp nutmeg
- ½ cup peanut butter, creamy
- 4 cups vegetable broth
- 1 tbsp ginger garlic paste
- 1 onion, diced
- Pepper
- Salt

Directions:

1. Add sweet potatoes and remaining ingredients into the slow cooker and stir well.
2. Cover and cook on low for 6 hours.
3. Puree the soup using a blender until smooth.
4. Stir well and serve.

Per serving: Calories: 201kcal; Fat: 1.3g; Carbs: 45g; Protein: 3.2g

101. Indian Vegetable Stew

Preparation time: 10 minutes

Cooking time: 3 to 4 hours

Servings: 4

Ingredients:

- 1 (15-oz/425-g) can of chickpeas, drained & rinsed
- 4 cups water
- 1 (15-ounce / 425-g) can no-salt-added diced tomatoes
- 2 medium sweet potatoes, peeled and diced
- 1 medium onion, diced
- 1 bell pepper, seeded and diced
- 2 garlic cloves, minced
- 1 tablespoon curry powder
- 1½ teaspoons ground ginger
- ½ teaspoon salt
- 1 teaspoon ground cumin

- 1 teaspoon ground turmeric
- 1 teaspoon ground coriander
- 1 teaspoon red pepper flakes
- ½ pint cherry tomatoes halved
- ½ cup frozen peas
- Chopped fresh parsley for garnish (optional)

Directions:

1. In the slow cooker, combine the chickpeas, water, tomatoes and their juices, sweet potatoes, onion, bell pepper, garlic, curry powder, ginger, salt, cumin, turmeric, coriander, and red pepper flakes. Stir to mix well.
2. Cook on low for 2½ to 3½ hours.
3. When there are 30 minutes left, stir in the cherry tomatoes and peas. Mix well and cook for the remaining 30 minutes.
4. Garnish with parsley (if using) and serve.

Per serving: Calories: 267kcal; Fat: 3g; Carbs: 51g; Protein: 12g

102. Savory Chicken and Watermelon Rind Soup

Preparation time: 10 minutes

Cooking time: 35 minutes

Servings: 4

Ingredients:

- 1 tablespoon olive oil
- ¾ pound (340 g) boneless, skinless chicken thighs
- 2 tablespoons minced garlic
- 1 teaspoon peeled minced fresh ginger
- Pinch sea salt
- Pinch freshly ground black pepper
- 6 cups water
- 3 cups diced watermelon rind

Directions:

1. In a huge stockpot, heat the olive oil over medium heat. Add the chicken, garlic,

ginger, salt, and pepper, and sauté until the chicken is no longer pink, about 5 minutes.

2. Add the water to the pot, increase the heat to high, and bring the soup to a boil.

3. Add the watermelon rind once the water comes to a boil.

4. Let the soup come to a boil again, reduce the heat to medium, and simmer for 30 minutes.

5. Add more salt, if desired, and enjoy immediately.

Per serving: Calories: 157kcal; Fat: 7g; Carbs: 6g; Protein: 17g

103. Spicy Lentil Chili

Preparation time: 10 minutes

Cooking time: 20 minutes

Servings: 4

Ingredients:

- 1 tablespoon olive oil
- 1 onion, chopped
- 5 cloves garlic, minced
- 1 jalapeño pepper, seeded and minced
- 1 cup red lentils, sorted and rinsed
- 1 tablespoon chili powder
- 1 teaspoon smoked paprika
- ⅛ teaspoon red pepper flakes
- 1 (14-ounce / 397-g) can no-salt-added diced tomatoes, undrained
- 3 tablespoons no-salt-added tomato paste
- 1 (16-ounce / 454-g) can of low-sodium kidney beans, rinsed and drained
- ⅓ cup chopped fresh cilantro leaves

Directions:

1. In a large saucepan, heat the olive oil over medium heat.

2. Add the onion, garlic, and jalapeño pepper, and cook and stir for 2 minutes.

3. Add the lentils, chili powder, paprika, red pepper flakes, tomatoes, tomato paste, and kidney beans, and bring to a boil.

4. Lower the heat, partially cover the pan, and simmer for 15 to 18 minutes until the chili powder has blended in and the lentils are tender. Top with the fresh cilantro and serve.

Per serving: Calories: 364kcal; Fat: 5g; Carbs: 59g; Protein: 22g

104. Hearty Vegetable Stew

Preparation time: 15 minutes

Cooking time: 25 minutes

Servings: 2

Ingredients:

- 2 teaspoons olive oil
- 2 celery stalks, chopped
- ½ sweet onion, peeled and chopped
- 1 teaspoon minced garlic
- 3 cups low-sodium vegetable broth
- 1 cup chopped tomatoes
- 2 carrots, thinly sliced
- 1 cup cauliflower florets
- 1 cup broccoli florets
- 1 yellow bell pepper, diced
- 1 cup low-sodium canned black beans, rinsed & drained
- Pinch red pepper flakes
- Sea salt, to taste
- Freshly ground black pepper
- 2 tablespoons grated low-fat Parmesan cheese for garnish
- 1 tablespoon chopped fresh parsley, for garnish

Directions:

1. In a large saucepan, warm the olive oil over medium-high heat.

2. Add celery, onions, and garlic, and sauté until softened, about 4 minutes.

3. Stir in the vegetable broth, tomatoes, carrots, cauliflower, broccoli, bell peppers, black beans, and red pepper flakes.

4. Bring the stew to a boil, then reduce the heat to low and simmer until the vegetables are tender, 18 to 20 minutes.

5. Season with salt and pepper.

6. Serve topped with Parmesan cheese and parsley.

Per serving: Calories: 270kcal; Fat: 8g; Carbs: 35g; Protein: 17g

105. Nutritious Scallop Shrimp Stew

Preparation time: 10 minutes

Cooking time: 3 hours

Servings: 6

Ingredients:

- 1 lb. scallops
- 1 lb. shrimp, peeled & deveined
- 1 tsp dried oregano
- 1 tsp dried basil
- 1 tsp dried thyme
- 1 medium onion, chopped
- 1 lb. potatoes, cut into 1-inch pieces
- 1 tbsp garlic, minced
- 4 cups vegetable broth
- 1 tbsp tomato puree
- 28 oz can tomato, crushed
- Pepper
- Salt

Directions:

1. Add all ingredients except scallops and shrimp into the slow cooker and stir well.

2. Cover and then cook on high for 2 hours.

3. Add scallops and shrimp and stir well.

4. Cover again and cook for 40-60 minutes or until shrimp and scallops are cooked.

5. Stir well and serve.

Per serving: Calories: 254kcal; Fat: 2.1g; Carbs: 25.1g; Protein: 33.1g

106. Seafood Stew

Preparation time: 10 minutes

Cooking time: 13 minutes

Servings: 2

Ingredients:

- 1/2 lb. shrimp, shelled and chopped
- 1/2 tsp garlic, chopped
- 1 yellow onion, chopped
- 1 tbsp olive oil
- 1 celery stalk, chopped
- 1/2 lb. crab meat
- 2 cups chicken broth
- Pepper
- Salt

Directions:

1. Add olive oil into the instant pot. Set pot on sauté mode.

2. Once the oil is hot, add onion, then sauté for 3 minutes.

3. Add garlic and sauté for 30 seconds. Turn off sauté mode.

4. Add remaining ingredients and stir everything well.

5. Cover and cook on high for 10 minutes.

6. Once cooking is done, then release the pressure manually. Remove lid.

7. Stir well and serve.

Per serving: Calories: 333kcal; Fat: 20g; Carbs: 7.3g; Protein: 48.1g

CHAPTER 8: Snacks

107. Berry Greek Yogurt Parfaits with Granola

Preparation time: 10 minutes

Cooking time: 0 minute

Servings: 5

Ingredients:

- 5 cups nonfat plain Greek yogurt
- 1 tbsp. ground cinnamon
- 10 tbsps. Super-Simple Granola or store-bought
- 2½ cups fresh berries (any kind), sliced if large

Directions:

1. In a medium bowl, stir together the Greek yogurt & cinnamon.
2. Evenly divide the yogurt into 5 storage containers. Distribute 2 tbsps. of granola and ½ cup of fresh berries in each container.

Per serving: Calories: 265kcal; Fat: 7g; Carbs: 26g; Protein: 27g

108. Thyme Mushrooms

Preparation time: 10 minutes

Cooking time: 30 minutes

Servings: 4

Ingredients:

- 1 tbsp of chopped thyme
- 2 tbsp of olive oil
- 2 tbsp of chopped parsley
- 4 garlic cloves, minced
- 1 tbsp of black pepper
- 2 lbs. of halved white mushrooms

Directions:

1. Preheat your oven to 400 deg. F.
2. In a baking pan, combine the mushrooms with the garlic and the other ingredients and toss,
3. Place in the oven and cook for 30 minutes.

4. Divide between plates and serve.

Per serving: Calories: 116kcal; Fat: 7.5g; Carbs: 9g; Protein: 7.5g

109. Nutritious Roasted Chickpeas

Preparation time: 10 minutes

Cooking time: 14 minutes

Servings: 2

Ingredients:

- 14 oz can chickpeas, drained & rinsed
- 1 tsp dried oregano
- 1 tsp dried thyme
- 1 tsp dried rosemary
- 2 tbsp sesame oil
- 1 ½ tsp onion powder
- Pepper
- Salt

Directions:

1. In a mixing bowl, toss chickpeas with oil, onion powder, rosemary, thyme, oregano, pepper, and salt until well coated.
2. Transfer chickpeas into the air fryer basket and cook at 370 F for 14 minutes. Stir halfway through.
3. Serve and enjoy.

Per serving: Calories: 369kcal; Fat: 16.5g; Carbs: 47.6g; Protein: 10.3g

110. Curried Cannellini Bean Dip

Preparation time: 10 minutes

Cooking time: 5 minutes

Servings: 4

Ingredients:

- 14 oz can cannellini beans, drained & rinsed
- 1 tbsp fresh lemon juice
- 3 tbsp water
- ½ tsp curry powder

- 2 garlic cloves
- 2 tbsp Sriracha sauce
- 1 ½ tsp tamari sauce
- 2 tbsp olive oil
- Salt

Directions:

1. Add cannellini beans and remaining ingredients into the blender and blend until smooth and creamy.
2. Serve and enjoy.

Per serving: Calories: 396kcal; Fat: 7.9g; Carbs: 60.6g; Protein: 23.7g

111. Crispy Carrot Fries

Preparation time: 10 minutes

Cooking time: 20 minutes

Servings: 4

Ingredients:

- 3 large carrots, peel & cut into fries' shape
- ½ tsp paprika
- ½ tsp onion powder
- 2 tbsp olive oil
- ¼ tsp chili powder
- 1 tsp garlic powder
- Pepper
- Salt

Directions:

1. Preheat your air fryer to 350 deg. F.
2. Tossing carrot fries with remaining ingredients in a mixing bowl until well coated.
3. Add carrot fries into the air fryer basket and cook for 15-20 minutes. Stir halfway through.
4. Serve and enjoy.

Per serving: Calories: 87kcal; Fat: 7.1g; Carbs: 6.3g; Protein: 0.7g

112. Cannellini Bean Hummus

Preparation time: 10 minutes

Cooking time: 5 minutes

Servings: 16

Ingredients:

- 30 oz can cannellini beans, drained & rinsed
- ¼ cup olive oil
- 1/8 tsp chili powder
- 1 tsp garlic powder
- 1 tsp cumin powder
- 3 tbsp fresh lemon juice
- ¼ cup water
- Salt

Directions:

1. Add beans and remaining ingredients into the food processor and process until desired consistency.
2. Serve and enjoy.

Per serving: Calories: 68kcal; Fat: 3.2g; Carbs: 9g; Protein: 3.1g

113. Black Bean Dip

Preparation time: 10 minutes

Cooking time: 5 minutes

Servings: 6

Ingredients:

- 14 oz can black beans, drained & rinsed
- ½ tsp cumin powder
- ¼ cup fresh lemon juice
- ¼ cup sesame oil
- ¼ cup tahini
- 4 garlic cloves
- Salt

Directions:

1. Add black beans and remaining ingredients into the blender and blend until desired consistency.
2. Serve and enjoy.

Per serving: Calories: 197kcal; Fat: 14.1g; Carbs: 14.7g; Protein: 5.4g

114. Healthy Beet Dip

Preparation time: 10 minutes

Cooking time: 5 minutes

Servings: 6

Ingredients:

- 2 large beets, roasted, peeled& chopped
- ½ cup sesame oil
- ¼ cup fresh lemon juice
- 1 ½ tbsp tahini
- 2 garlic cloves
- 2 tbsp almond flour
- 1 tsp cumin powder
- 1 ¼ cups walnuts
- Salt

Directions:

1. Add chopped beets and remaining ingredients into the blender and blend until desired consistency.
2. Serve and enjoy.

Per serving: Calories: 357kcal; Fat: 35.4g; Carbs: 7.3g; Protein: 8g

115. Homemade Lemony Tomato Salsa

Preparation time: 8 minutes

Cooking time: 10 minutes

Servings: 2½ cups

Ingredients:

- 2 cups chopped tomatoes (about 2 medium tomatoes)
- ½ cup diced red onion (about ½ medium onion)
- 1 jalapeño, seeded and chopped
- ⅛ cup minced basil
- 1 tsp. minced garlic (about 2 small cloves)
- 1 tsp. ground rosemary
- 1½ tbsps. lemon juice (about ½ small lemon)
- Salt and pepper to taste

Directions:

1. Puree all the ingredients on high in a food processor until smooth.

Per serving: Calories: 39kcal; Fat: 0.4g; Carbs: 9.2g; Protein: 1.5g

116. Easy Lentil Dip

Preparation time: 10 minutes

Cooking time: 5 minutes

Servings: 4

Ingredients:

- 1 cup cooked lentils
- 1 tsp onion powder
- 2 tbsp vegetable broth
- 2 tbsp peanut butter
- 3 garlic cloves
- 2 tbsp lemon basil vinegar
- 4 tbsp walnuts

Directions:

1. Add cooked lentils and remaining ingredients into the blender and blend until desired consistency.
2. Serve and enjoy.

Per serving: Calories: 285kcal; Fat: 9.7g; Carbs: 33.8g; Protein: 16.9g

117. Caprese Skewers

Preparation time: 5 minutes

Cooking time: 0 minute

Servings: 2

Ingredients:

- 12 red tomatoes
- 2 red bell peppers
- 12 basil leaves
- 8 (1-inch) pieces of ricotta cheese
- ¼ cup Italian Vinaigrette (optional for serving)

Directions:

1. Thread the following onto each of four wooden skewers: 1 tomato, 1 basil leaf, 1 mozzarella cube, 1 tomato, and 1 red bell

pepper 1 basil leaf, 1 cheese cube, 1 basil leaf, and 1 tomato

2. If desired, serve with vinaigrette for dipping.

Per serving: Calories: 338kcal; Fat: 24g; Carbs: 6gProtein: 25g

118. Winter Perfect Guacamole

Preparation time: 10 minutes

Cooking time: 5 minutes

Servings: 8

Ingredients:

- 3 avocados, peel, pitted & chopped
- 1 jalapeno pepper, seeded & minced
- 1 tsp garlic, chopped
- ½ tsp cumin
- 1 ½ tbsp fresh lemon juice
- 2 tbsp fresh parsley, chopped
- 1 large pear, core & chopped
- Pepper
- Salt

Directions:

1. In a mixing bowl, mix chopped avocado and the remaining ingredients.
2. Serve and enjoy.

Per serving: Calories: 166kcal; Fat: 14.8g; Carbs: 9.4g; Protein: 1.6g

119. Refreshing Cucumber Salsa

Preparation time: 10 minutes

Cooking time: 5 minutes

Servings: 4

Ingredients:

- 2 medium cucumbers, chopped
- 2 tbsp fresh lime juice
- ½ tbsp olive oil
- ¼ cup fresh cilantro, chopped
- 2 tbsp jalapeno, chopped
- 1 medium onion, chopped
- 4 peaches, chopped

- Pepper
- Salt

Directions:

1. In a mixing bowl, mix chopped cucumbers and the remaining ingredients.
2. Serve immediately and enjoy.

Per serving: Calories: 112kcal; Fat: 2.5g; Carbs: 22.6g; Protein: 2.9g

120. Creamy Avocado Chickpea Hummus

Preparation time: 10 minutes

Cooking time: 5 minutes

Servings: 4

Ingredients:

- 14 oz can chickpeas, rinsed & drained
- 2 tbsp olive oil
- ½ tsp ground coriander
- 2 garlic cloves
- 1 tsp sesame seed paste
- ¼ cup water
- ¼ cup fresh cilantro
- 2 avocados, scoop out the flesh
- Salt

Directions:

1. Add chickpeas and remaining ingredients into the blender and blend until smooth.
2. Serve and enjoy.

Per serving: Calories: 392kcal; Fat: 28.2g; Carbs: 32.1g; Protein: 7.2g

121. Avocado Tomato Salsa

Preparation time: 10 minutes

Cooking time: 5 minutes

Servings: 4

Ingredients:

- 4 avocados, peel, core & chopped
- 5 large tomatoes, chopped
- ½ cup fresh cilantro, chopped
- 1 ½ lime juice

- 1 jalapeno pepper, seeded & chopped
- 1 small onion, chopped
- Salt

Directions:

1. Add tomatoes, avocado, onion, jalapeno pepper, lime juice, and cilantro into the mixing bowl and mix well—season with salt.
2. Serve and enjoy.

Per serving: Calories: 466kcal; Fat: 39.9g; Carbs: 28.8g; Protein: 6.4g

CHAPTER 9: Desserts

122. Watermelon Berry Ice Pops

Preparation time: 5 minutes

Cooking time: 5 minutes

Servings: 6

Ingredients:

- 8 oz watermelon, seeded & chopped
- 1 lime juice
- 4 oz raspberries
- 4 oz strawberries

Directions:

1. Add watermelon, lime juice, and berries into the blender and blend until smooth.
2. Pour watermelon mixture into the popsicle molds and place in the refrigerator until set.
3. Serve chilled and enjoy.

Per serving: Calories: 29kcal; Fat: 0.3g; Carbs: 6.7g; Protein: 0.6g

123. Chocolate Mousse

Preparation time: 10 minutes

Cooking time: 5 minutes

Servings: 4

Ingredients:

- 3 avocados, scoop out the flesh
- 1 ½ tbsp agave syrup
- 1 tsp vanilla
- 1/3 cup unsweetened soy milk
- ¼ cup unsweetened cocoa powder
- 1 oz semi-sweet chocolate, chopped
- 2 dates pitted
- Pinch of salt

Directions:

1. Add chopped chocolate into the microwave-safe bowl and microwave for 30 seconds. Stir well.
2. Pour melted chocolate and remaining ingredients into the blender and blend until smooth.
3. Serve and enjoy.

Per serving: Calories: 391kcal; Fat: 32.1g; Carbs: 28.9g; Protein: 4.4g

124. Refreshing Watermelon Ice Pops

Preparation time: 5 minutes

Cooking time: 5 minutes

Servings: 12

Ingredients:

- 4 cups watermelon
- 2 tbsp fresh mint, chopped

Directions:

1. Add watermelon into the blender and blend until smooth. Add mint and stir well.
2. Pour watermelon mixture into the popsicle molds and place in the refrigerator until set.
3. Serve chilled and enjoy.

Per serving: Calories: 16kcal; Fat: 0.1g; Carbs: 3.9g; Protein: 0.3g

125. Baked Apple Slices

Preparation time: 10 minutes

Cooking time: 30 minutes

Servings: 4

Ingredients:

- 4 medium apples, core & slice
- ¼ tsp ground cinnamon
- ¼ tsp ground nutmeg
- 1 tbsp coconut oil, melted

Directions:

1. Preheat the oven to 375 F.
2. Add apple slices into the baking dish, drizzle with coconut oil, and sprinkle with cinnamon and nutmeg.
3. Bake for 25-30 minutes.

4. Serve and enjoy.

Per serving: Calories: 146kcal; Fat: 3.9g; Carbs: 31g; Protein: 0.6g

126. Creamy Delicious Farro

Preparation time: 10 minutes
Cooking time: 30 minutes
Servings: 4
Ingredients:

- 1 cup farro, rinsed & drained
- 6 dates, pitted & chopped
- ½ tsp cardamom powder
- 1 tsp vanilla
- 2 cups water
- 1 cup unsweetened soy milk

Directions:

1. Heat water & almond milk in a saucepan over high heat.
2. Once boiling starts, add dates, farro, cardamom powder, and vanilla and cook for 25-30 minutes over low heat.
3. Stir well and serve.

Per serving: Calories: 142kcal; Fat: 5g; Carbs: 22.1g; Protein: 4.6g

127. Brown Rice Pudding

Preparation time: 10 minutes
Cooking time: 4 hours
Servings: 4
Ingredients:

- ½ cup brown rice, rinsed
- ¼ cup raisins
- ¼ cup walnuts, chopped
- 1 ½ tsp cinnamon
- 2 tbsp agave syrup
- 1 tsp vanilla
- 1 ½ cup unsweetened almond milk
- 1 ½ cup unsweetened coconut milk
- Pinch of salt

Directions:

1. Add rice, walnuts, cinnamon, agave syrup, vanilla, almond milk, coconut milk, and salt into the slow cooker and stir well.
2. Cover and then cook on low for 4 hours.
3. Add raisins and stir well.
4. Serve and enjoy.

Per serving: Calories: 401kcal; Fat: 26.5g; Carbs: 39.8g; Protein: 5.8g

128. Mango Shake

Preparation time: 5 minutes
Cooking time: 0 minutes
Servings: 4
Ingredients:

- 2 cups low-fat milk
- 4 tablespoons frozen mango juice (or 1 fresh mango, pitted)
- 1 small banana
- 2 ice cubes

Directions:

1. Put all ingredients into a blender. Blend until foamy. Serve immediately.

Per serving: Calories: 106kcal; Fat: 2g; Carbs: 20g; Protein: 5g

129. Summer Breezes Smoothie

Preparation time: 5 minutes
Cooking time: 0 minutes
Servings: 3
Ingredients:

- 1 cup fat-free plain yogurt
- 1 cup pineapple, crushed and canned in juice
- 6 medium strawberries
- 1 medium banana
- 1 teaspoon vanilla extract
- 4 ice cubes

Directions:

1. Place all ingredients in blender and purée until smooth.
2. Serve in frosted glass.

Per serving: Calories: 121kcal; Fat: 0g; Carbs: 24g; Protein: 6g

130. Peanut Butter and Chocolate Black Bean Brownie

Preparation time: 10 minutes

Cooking time: 15 minutes

Servings: 6

Ingredients:

- 1 (15-ounce / 425-g) can of low-sodium black beans, drained and rinsed
- 6 small dates, halved
- 1½ ounces (43 g) 70% dark chocolate bar, quartered
- 2 tablespoons quick-cooking oats
- 2 tablespoons unsalted raw peanut butter
- 2 tablespoons water

Directions:

1. Preheat the oven to 350 deg. F.
2. In a medium bowl for a food processor, combine the black beans, dates, chocolate, oats, peanut butter, and water. Blend until very smooth and doughy, 2 to 3 minutes.
3. Pour the batter into an 8-inch square baking pan and spread evenly. Cook for about 15 minutes until the top turns a darker brown, is cracked, and a fork comes out clean when inserted in the middle.
4. Cool for at least 5 mins before cutting into 6 squares. Store in an airtight container for up to 3 days on the counter.

Per serving: Calories: 160kcal; Fat: 6g; Carbs: 22g; Protein: 6g

131. Banana Cream Nonfat Yogurt

Preparation time: 3 minutes

Cooking time: 0 minute

Servings: 1

Ingredients:

- 1 medium banana
- 1 graham cracker
- 1 tsp. fresh lemon juice
- 1 cup nonfat vanilla yogurt

Directions:

1. Slice the banana into a bowl.
2. Break the graham cracker into small pieces and add to the banana.
3. Sprinkle with lemon juice and top with yogurt.

Per serving: Calories: 125kcal; Fat: 1.56g; Carbs: 10.29g; Protein: 17.64g

Conversion Chart

Volume Equivalents (Liquid)

US Standard	US Standard (ounces)	Metric (approximate)
2 tablespoons	1 fl. oz.	30 mL
¼ cup	2 fl. oz.	60 mL
½ cup	4 fl. oz.	120 mL
1 cup	8 fl. oz.	240 mL
1½ cups	12 fl. oz.	355 mL
2 cups or 1 pint	16 fl. oz.	475 mL
4 cups or 1 quart	32 fl. oz.	1 L
1 gallon	128 fl. oz.	4 L

Volume Equivalents (Dry)

US Standard	Metric (approximate)
⅛ teaspoon	0.5 mL
¼ teaspoon	1 mL
½ teaspoon	2 mL
¾ teaspoon	4 mL
1 teaspoon	5 mL
1 tablespoon	15 mL
¼ cup	59 mL
⅓ cup	79 mL
½ cup	118 mL
⅔ cup	156 mL
¾ cup	177 mL
1 cup	235 mL
2 cups or 1 pint	475 mL
3 cups	700 mL
4 cups or 1 quart	1 L

Oven Temperatures

Fahrenheit (F)	Celsius (C) (approximate)
250°F	120°C
300°F	150°C
325°F	165°C
350°F	180°C
375°F	190°C
400°F	200°C
425°F	220°C
450°F	230°C

Weight Equivalents

US Standard	Metric (approximate)
½ ounce	15 g
1 ounce	30 g
2 ounces	60 g
4 ounces	115 g
8 ounces	225 g
12 ounces	340 g
16 ounces or 1 pound	455 g

30-Day Meal Plan

Days	Breakfast	Lunch	Dinner	Dessert
1	Breakfast Cereal With Apples And Raisins	Sautéed Spinach With Pumpkin Seeds	Salmon Wrap	Chocolate Mousse
2	Creamy Oats Banana Porridge	Chicken Shaheata	Cauliflower Mashed "Potatoes"	Black Bean Dip
3	Peach-Cranberry Sunrise Muesli	Chopped Tuna Salad	Hot Chicken Wings	Creamy Delicious Farro
4	Roasted Pears With Walnuts	Buckwheat With Potatoes And Kale	Rosemary-Lemon Salmon	Easy Lentil Dip
5	Delicious Blueberry Smoothie	Tasty Chicken Wings	Grilled Cauliflower With Spicy Lentil Sauce	Summer Breezes Smoothie
6	Delicious Breakfast Barley	Baked Fish Served With Vegetables	Delicious Chicken Tenders	Creamy Avocado Chickpea Hummus
7	Healthy Overnight Oatmeal	Slow Cooker Quinoa Lentil Tacos	Steamed Veggie And Lemon Pepper Salmon	Banana Cream Nonfat Yogurt
8	Peanut Butter Brazilian Nut Smoothie Bowl	Juicy Chicken Breast	Sesame Spinach	Homemade Lemony Tomato Salsa
9	Muesli With Berries, Seeds, And Nuts	Stewed Cod Filet With Tomatoes	Grill Lemon Chicken	Brown Rice Pudding
10	Strawberry Yogurt Tarts	Vegetable Fruit Bowl With Lentil	Lemon Salmon With Kaffir Lime	Nutritious Roasted Chickpeas
11	Red Velvet Beet And Cherry Smoothie	Chicken With Orzo And Lemon	Spaghetti Squash With Walnuts And Parmesan	Refreshing Watermelon Ice Pops
12	Berry, Walnut, And Cinnamon Quinoa Bowl	Sardine Bruschetta With Fennel And Lemon Crema	Juicy Chicken Patties	Thyme Mushrooms
13	Cereal Cream With Flaxseed And Fruit	Healthy Cauliflower Purée	Crispy Trout With Herb	Watermelon Berry Ice Pops
14	Sweet Potatoes With Pineapple	Creamy Chicken Salad	Almond Noodles With Cauliflower	Crispy Carrot Fries
15	Beet Berry Smoothie	Green Goddess Crab Salad With Endive	Italian Chicken Skewers	Baked Apple Slices

16	Protein Packed Quinoa	Sweet Spot Lentil Salad	Grilled Halibut And Fruit Salsa	Healthy Beet Dip
17	Quinoa Bowl With Blackberry	Amazing Grilled Chicken And Blueberry Salad	Perfect Sweet Potatoes	Peanut Butter And Chocolate Black Bean Brownie
18	Hummus And Date Bagel	Flounder With Tomatoes And Basil	Sweet & Tangy Chicken	Winter Perfect Guacamole
19	Orange Apricot Muesli	Easy Basic Table Salad	Mediterranean Baked Fish	Mango Shake
20	Tasty Cherry Smoothie	Asian Chicken Breasts	Vegetable Kabobs	Cannellini Bean Hummus
21	Muesli With Berries, Seeds, And Nuts	Spicy Cod	Healthy Turkey Salad	Watermelon Berry Ice Pops
22	Strawberry Yogurt Tarts	Umami Mushrooms	Creamy Haddock With Kale	Avocado Tomato Salsa
23	Red Velvet Beet And Cherry Smoothie	Coconut Curry Sea Bass	Spicy Chicken	Chocolate Mousse
24	Berry, Walnut, And Cinnamon Quinoa Bowl	Chicken Tikka	Garlic And Tomatoes On Mussels	Refreshing Cucumber Salsa
25	Creamy Oats Banana Porridge	Ginger Sesame Salmon	Herb Chicken Breast	Brown Rice Pudding
26	Peach-Cranberry Sunrise Muesli	Meatballs	Easy Shrimp	Curried Cannellini Bean Dip
27	Roasted Pears With Walnuts	Spicy Shrimp	Hearty Chicken Stew	Baked Apple Slices
28	Delicious Blueberry Smoothie	Garlic Mushroom Chicken	Chicken Shaheata	Caprese Skewers
29	Healthy Overnight Oatmeal	Chicken With Orzo And Lemon	Spaghetti Squash With Walnuts And Parmesan	Peanut Butter And Chocolate Black Bean Brownie
30	Peanut Butter Brazilian Nut Smoothie Bowl	Sardine Bruschetta With Fennel And Lemon Crema	Juicy Chicken Patties	Berry Greek Yogurt Parfaits With Granola

Conclusion

The heart is a symbol of love, but the sad reality is that most people don't give their heart the kind of love it deserves. Consider the fact that heart disease is currently a leading cause of death. That's a sobering reality. However, by taking preventive steps such as following a heart-healthy diet, you can improve your chances of beating the odds.

A healthy heart lifestyle can be fun, delicious, and empowering, or it can seem overwhelming and restrictive. To achieve success and have some fun doing it, stop and consider the mindset you bring to this transition. Then cultivate approaches that keep your motivation high.

One way to support yourself is by practicing mindfulness. Mindfulness is a way of paying attention to what you are experiencing each moment. Thoughts like "I don't have time to take care of myself with nourishing foods," or "I never make good choices," can derail you from reaching your goals, but when you become aware of these kinds of entirely normal but self-defeating thoughts, you have more power over them. Self-compassion can begin to free you from old ways of thinking. Instead of automatically following through on those negative thoughts, decide to veto your thoughts and choose a different course of action.

How does this work regarding eating? In this case, mindfulness helps you gain insight into how you talk to yourself and the impulses driving your eating choices. This exercise will support you in breaking old habits and transitioning to foods that keep you fueled in a sustained and lasting way. And it will eventually become natural. Imagine how great you will feel in light of all this positive change—you broke old habits, achieved success, and improved your health! As time goes on, your mindfulness practice will help you be more aware of how energized and steady you feel when you nourish yourself this way.

By taking time to sit and thoughtfully enjoy your food, you can use mindful eating to check in with yourself anytime you eat. It becomes a more powerful tool when you practice it regularly.

Thank you for reading this book. I wish you all the best!

Index

Potato Squash Soup; 50
Protein Packed Quinoa; 20
Quinoa Bowl with Blackberry; 19
Red Velvet Beet and Cherry Smoothie; 16
Refreshing Cucumber Salsa; 59
Refreshing Watermelon Ice Pops; 61
Roasted Broccoli Salad; 24
Roasted Brussels sprouts; 26
Roasted Pears with Walnuts; 20
Roasted Sweet Carrots; 23
Rosemary-Lemon Salmon; 42
Salmon Wrap; 43
Sardine Bruschetta with Fennel and Lemon Crema; 44
Sautéed Garlic Mushrooms; 26
Sautéed Spinach with Pumpkin Seeds; 28
Savory Chicken and Watermelon Rind Soup; 53
Seafood Stew; 55
Sesame Spinach; 29
Silky Zucchini Soup; 51
Slow Cooker Quinoa Lentil Tacos; 33
Spaghetti Squash with Walnuts and Parmesan; 28
Spicy Chicken; 38

Spicy Cod; 46
Spicy Lentil Chili; 54
Spicy Shrimp; 49
Steamed Veggie and Lemon Pepper Salmon; 47
Stewed Cod Filet with Tomatoes; 48
Strawberry Yogurt Tarts; 18
Summer Breezes Smoothie; 62
Sweet & Tangy Chicken; 40
Sweet Potatoes with Pineapple; 20
Sweet Spot Lentil Salad; 29
Tasty Cherry Smoothie; 21
Tasty Chicken Wings; 37
Thick & Creamy Potato Soup; 52
Thyme Mushrooms; 56
Tofu with Brussels sprouts; 25
Tomato and Avocado Salad; 23
Turmeric Peppers Platter; 27
Tuscan Fish Stew; 52
Umami Mushrooms; 29
Vegetable Fruit Bowl with Lentil; 33
Vegetable Kabobs; 30
Watermelon Berry Ice Pops; 61
Winter Perfect Guacamole; 59